SEI
OF HORROR
AND SUSPENSE

Bram (Abraham) Stoker (1847-1912), novelist, short story and non-fiction writer, was born in Clontarf, Ireland, on November 8th, 1847, the third of seven children born into a Protestant Irish family. His father was civil servant Abraham Stoker (1799-1876) and his mother was Charlotte Mathilda Blake Thorney (1818-1901). Charlotte, who was considerably younger than her husband, is remembered as an early feminist.

Bram was a sickly child who spent the first years of his childhood bedridden. The nature of his illness, like much of his life, is a mystery, but he appears to have recovered by the time he started school at the age of around seven. It is believed that during his illness his mother would often entertain him with stories, many of which were vivid and gruesome accounts of her experiences during a terrible cholera epidemic that reached her home town of Sligo in 1832. These tales are thought to have had a profound influence on Stoker, awakening a dark side of his imagination and later being echoed in much of his writing. Stoker's early ill health does not appear to have had lasting effects. As a young man, tall and vigorous, he excelled as a scholar, debater and sportsman at Trinity College in Dublin, where he studied history, literature, mathematics and physics, earning both an honours degree in science and a masters degree in mathematics.

During his student years, Stoker became interested in the theatre. While working as a civil servant after leaving college, he developed this interest further, becoming the theatre critic of the *Dublin Evening Mail*, a newspaper co-owned by Joseph

Sheridan Le Fanu (1814-1873). Le Fanu was a journalist and writer with a particular interest in the supernatural and his novella *Carmilla*, published in the short story collection *In a Glass Darkly* (1872), is thought to have provided Stoker with much inspiration for his defining novel *Dracula* (1897).

In 1876 Stoker saw leading actor of the time, Henry Irving, playing the title role in *Hamlet* at Dublin's Theatre Royal. Hugely impressed by Irving, he wrote a glowing account of the actor's performance. As a result of this, the two men met and became firm friends. Indeed, Stoker so admired the actor that he would later name first son, and only child, after him. Stoker went on to develop business relations with Irving, becoming his personal assistant, and also, for nearly thirty years, manager of the actor's Lyceum Theatre in London.

In 1878, Stoker married Florence Balcombe, a renowned society beauty previously linked romantically with Oscar Wilde. Bram Stoker already knew Wilde from their college days at Trinity and also through a friendship with Wilde's parents. It is said that Wilde's disappointment over the loss of Florence led him to abandon Dublin shortly after the announcement of her engagement to Bram. Despite this, Stoker and Wilde were later reconciled. Because of Stoker's work with Irving, Bram and Florence moved to London after their marriage. Their only child, a son named Irving Noel Thornley Stoker, was born on December 31st, 1879.

Stoker's deep friendship and collaboration with Irving was to prove the key influence in his life. Through his association with the actor he travelled widely. Twice a guest at the White House, he was favourably impressed with America and met important personages there, including US presidents Theodore Roosevelt and William McKinley, and poet and writer Walt Whitman, whom he particularly admired. In London, he mixed with members of high society and with important literary and artistic figures, including Arthur Conan Doyle and Alfred Lord Tennyson.

When, in 1905, Irving died, Stoker was devastated and a stroke he suffered soon after Irving's death has been attributed to his grief. The following year Stoker published *Personal Reminiscences of Henry Irving*, a biography of his great friend.

In his later years Stoker suffered a number of strokes. He finally died on April 20th, 1912. The cause of his death is disputed, some biographers attributing it to syphilis, others to a stroke.

Florence outlived Bram by twenty-five years and, after the author's death, became his literary executor.

Bram Stoker

LITERARY PROFILE

Bram Stoker began writing novels and short stories while still at college and continued to do so during his eight years as a civil servant working at Dublin Castle. In this period he regularly contributed short stories to different periodicals.
Subsequently, while earning his living as a journalist, and also as personal assistant to actor Sir Henry Irving and manager of Irving's London-based theatre, he continued to write, encouraged in his literary endeavours by the success of his first novel *The Snake's Pass* (1890).
Although Stoker wrote prolifically and in different genres (magazine reviews, stories, novels, non-fiction), he is known almost exclusively, the world over, as the author of *Dracula* (1897), one of the first and certainly the most famous horror novel ever written. Whereas few people are familiar with Stoker's other novels, which have been criticized for being excessively melodramatic and for featuring rigidly stereotyped characters, *Dracula* has remained in print ever since it was first published and is universally known, thanks in part to numerous film and theatre adaptations of the story. Far from being the first-ever story of vampirism, *Dracula* is, by many, regarded as the Gothic vampire tale par excellence, being the ultimate expression of a centuries-old literary and mythical tradition.
Dracula is an epistolary novel, constructed as a collection of diary entries, letters, newspaper clippings and so on, apparently compiled by the novel's protagonist, young English lawyer Jonathan Harker. This is a well-known literary stratagem, designed to lend an aura of realism to a narrative that might otherwise sound incredible.
Stoker was interested in the supernatural and the occult and is alleged to have participated in magic circles, although there is no definite evidence to support this claim. However, he had little time for superstition and, as a scientist, carefully researched aspects of his most famous novel, e.g. the folklore and geography of areas such as the Balkans and Eastern Europe, where many European vampire legends originated.
Dracula can be read on a number of levels, religious, medical, and political. Like Le Fanu's *Carmilla*, it has also often been interpreted in Freudian psychosexual terms. *Dracula* was generally well received, although it was not without its critics, who seemed concerned that it might be disturbing for readers

of a delicate disposition. Bram Stoker's mother Charlotte particularly liked the book and on its publication predicted, accurately, that it would be a great success.

Stoker's short stories of horror, mystery and suspense, although little known singly, often feature in collections of horror stories. All but one of the stories included in this volume come from the collection *Dracula's Guest and Other Weird Stories* (1914), which was published posthumously by Stoker's wife two years after his death. Florence decided to add the first and title story *Dracula's Guest* to a collection her husband had been planning at the time he died. In the preface to the collection she describes this story as a 'hitherto unpublished episode from *Dracula* [...] originally excised owing to the length of the book'. She included it believing that it 'may prove of interest to the many readers of what is considered my husband's most remarkable work'.

WORKS

Novels

The Snake's Pass (1890)
Dracula (1897)
The Mystery of the Sea (1902)
The Jewel of Seven Stars (1903)
The Man (1905)
The Lady of the Shroud (1909)
The Lair of the White Worm (1911)

Short Story Collections

Under the Sunset (1881)
- *Under the Sunset*
- *The Rose Prince*
- *The Invisible Giant*
- *The Shadow Builder*
- *How 7 Went Mad*
- *Lies and Lilies*
- *The Castle of the King*
- *The Wondrous Child*

Dracula's Guest and Other Weird Stories (1914)
- *Dracula's Guest*
- *The Judge's House*
- *The Squaw*
- *The Secret of the Growing Gold*
- *The Gipsy Prophecy*
- *The Coming of Abel Behenna*
- *The Burial of the Rats*
- *A Dream of Red Hands*
- *Crooken Sands*

Uncollected Short Stories
- *The Crystal Cup*
- *The Chain of Destiny*
- *The Dualitists; or, The Death Doom of the Double Born*
- *The Red Stockade*
- *Bridal of Dead (alternative ending to The Jewel of Seven Stars)*
- *Buried Treasures*
- *The Fate of Fenella*
- *In the Valley of the Shadow*
- *The Man from Shorrox*
- *The Seer*

Non-fiction

The Duties of Clerks of Petty Sessions in Ireland (1879)
A Glimpse of America (1886)
Famous Impostors (1910)
Personal Reminiscences of Henry Irving (1906), a biography

THE CASTLE OF THE KING

When they told the poor Poet that the One he loved best was lying sick in the shadow of danger, he was nigh[1] distraught. For weeks past he had been alone; she, his Wife, having gone afar to her old home to see an aged grandsire[2] ere[3] he died. The Poet's heart had for some days been oppressed with a strange sorrow.

He did not know the cause of it; he only knew with the deep sympathy which is the poet's gift, that the One he loved was sick. Anxiously had he awaited tidings.

When the news came, the shock, although he expected a sad message, was too much for him, and he became nigh distraught. In his sadness and anxiety he went out into the garden which long years he had cultured for Her.

There, amongst the bright flowers, where the old statues stood softly white against the hedges of yew, he lay down in the long uncut summer grass, and wept with his head buried low. He thought of all the past – of how he had won his Wife and how they loved each other; and to him it seemed a sad and cruel thing that she was afar and in danger, and he not near to comfort her or even to share her pain. Many many thoughts came back to him, telling the story of the weary years whose gloom and solitude he had forgotten in the brightness of his lovely home. How in youth they twain had met and in a moment loved.

How his poverty and her greatness had kept them apart.

How he had struggled and toiled in the steep and rugged road to fame and fortune. How all through the weary years he had striven with the single idea of winning such a place in the history of his time, that he should be able to come and to her say, 'I love you,' and to her proud relations, 'I am worthy, for I too have become great.' How amid all this dreaming of a happy time which might come, he had kept silent as to his love.

How he had never seen her or heard her voice, or even known her habitation, lest, knowing, he should fail in the

---

[1] nigh *(archaic, poetic): near,* here, *almost*
[2] grandsire *(archaic): grandfather*
[3] ere *(archaic): before*

purpose of his life. How time – as it ever does to those who work with honesty and singleness of purpose – crowned the labours and the patience of his life. How the world had come to know his name and reverence and love it as of one who had helped the weak and weary by his example; who had purified the thoughts of all who listened to his words; and who had swept away baseness before the grandeur and simpleness of his noble thoughts. How success had followed in the wake of fame. How at length even to his heart, timorous with the doubt of love, had been borne the thought that he had at last achieved the greatness which justified him in seeking the hand of her he loved. How he had come back to his native place, and there found her still free. How when he had dared to tell her of his love she had whispered to him that she, too, had waited all the years, for that she knew that he would come to claim her at the end. How she had come with him as his bride into the home which he had been making for her all these years.

How, there, they had lived happily; and had dared to look into the long years to come for joy and content without a bar. How he thought that even then, when though somewhat enfeebled in strength by the ceaseless toil of years and the care of hoping, he might look to the happy time to come. But, alas! for hope; for who knoweth what a day may bring forth? Only a little while ago his Dear One had left him hale, departing in the cause of duty; and now she lay sick and he not nigh to help her. All the sunshine of his life seemed passing away.

All the long years of waiting and the patient continuance in well-doing which had crowned their years with love, seemed as but a passing dream, and was all in vain – all, all in vain. Now with the shadow hovering over his Beloved One, the cloud seemed to be above and around them, and to hold in its dim recesses the doom of them both. 'Why, oh why,' asked the poor Poet to the viewless air, 'did love come to us? Why came peace and joy and happiness, if the darkening wings of peril shadow the air around her, and leave me to weep alone?' Thus he moaned, and raved, and wept; and the bitter hours went by him in his solitude. As he lay in the garden with his face buried in the long grass, they came to him and told him with weeping, that tidings – sad, indeed – had come. As they spoke he lifted his poor head and gazed at them; and they saw in the great, dark, tender eyes that now he was quite distraught.

He smiled at them sadly, as though not quite understanding the import of their words.

As tenderly as they could they tried to tell him that the One he loved best was dead. They said: 'She has walked in the Valley of the Shadow;' but he seemed to understand them not. They whispered: 'She has heard the Music of the Spheres,' but still he comprehended not. Then they spoke to him sorrowfully and said: 'She now abides in the Castle of the King.'

He looked at them eagerly, as if to ask: 'What castle? What king?' They bowed their heads; and as they turned away weeping they murmured to him softly: 'The Castle of the King of Death.'

He spake[4] no word; so they turned their weeping faces to him again. They found that he had risen and stood with a set purpose on his face. Then he said sweetly: 'I go to find her, that where she abideth[5], I too may there abide.'

They said to him: 'You cannot go. Beyond the Portal she is, and in the Land of Death.'

Set purpose shone in the Poet's earnest, loving eyes as he answered them for the last time: 'Where she has gone, there go I too. Through the Valley of the Shadow shall I wend my way. In these ears also shall ring the Music of the Spheres. I shall seek, and I shall find my Beloved in the Halls of the Castle of the King. I shall clasp her close – even before the dread face of the King of Death.'

As they heard these words they bowed their heads again and wept, and said: 'Alas! alas!'

The Poet turned and left them; and passed away.

They fain would have followed; but he motioned them that they should not stir. So, alone, in his grief he went.

As he passed on he turned and waved his hand to them in farewell.

Then for a while with uplifted hand he stood, and turned him slowly all around. Suddenly his outstretched hand stopped and pointed.

---

[4] spake *(archaic): spoke*
[5] abideth *(archaic): abides*

His friends looking with him saw, where, away beyond the Portal, the idle wilderness spread.

There in the midst of desolation the mist from the marshes hung like a pall of gloom on the far-off horizon. As the Poet pointed there was a gleam of happiness – very faint it was – in his poor sad eyes, distraught with loss, as if afar he beheld some sign or hope of the Lost One.

Swiftly and sadly the Poet fared on through the burning day. The Rest Time came; but on he journeyed.

He paused not for shade or rest. Never, even for an instant did he stop to cool his parched lips with an icy draught from the crystal springs. The weary wayfarers resting in the cool shadows beside the fountains raised their tired heads and looked at him with sleepy eyes as he hurried.

He heeded them not; but went ever onwards with set purpose in his eyes, as though some gleam of hope bursting through the mists of the distant marshes urged him on. So he fared on through all the burning day, and all the silent night.

In the earliest dawn, when the promise of the still unrisen sun quickened the eastern sky into a pale light, he drew anigh the Portal.

The horizon stood out blackly in the cold morning light. There, as ever, stood the Angels who kept watch and ward, and oh, wondrous! although invisible to human eyes, they were seen of him. As he drew nigh they gazed at him pityingly and swept their great wings out wide, as if to shelter him.

He spake; and from his troubled heart the sad words came sweetly through the pale lips: 'Say, Ye[6] who guard the Land, has my Beloved One passed hither[7] on the journey to the Valley of the Shadow, to hear the Music of the Spheres, and to abide in the Castle of the King?' The Angels at the Portal bowed their heads in token of assent; and they turned and looked outwards from the Land to where, far off in the idle wilderness, the dank mists crept from the lifeless bosom of the marsh. They knew well that the poor lonely Poet was

---

[6] ye *(archaic): you*
[7] hither: *(archaic):* here, *this way*

in quest of his Beloved One; so they hindered him not, neither urged they him to stay.

They pitied him much for that much he loved. They parted wide, that through the Portal he might pass without let. So, the Poet went onwards into the idle desert to look for his Beloved One in the Castle of the King. For a time he went through gardens whose beauty was riper than the gardens of the Land.

The sweetness of all things stole on the senses like the odours from the Isles of the Blest. The subtlety of the King of Death, who rules in the Realms of Evil, is great.

He has ordered that the way beyond the Portal be made full of charm.

Thus those straying from the paths ordained for good see around them such beauty that in its joy the gloom and cruelty and guilt of the desert are forgotten. But as the Poet passed onwards the beauty began to fade away. The fair gardens looked as gardens do when the hand of care is taken off, and when the weeds in their hideous luxuriance choke, as they spring up, the choicer life of the flowers. From cool alleys under spreading branches, and from crisp sward which touched as soft as velvet the Wanderer's aching feet, the way became a rugged stony path, full open to the burning glare.

The flowers began to lose their odour, and to dwarf to stunted growth. Tall hemlocks rose on every side, infecting the air with their noisome odour. Great fungi grew in the dark hollows where the pools of dank water lay. Tall trees, with branches like skeletons, rose-trees which had no leaves, and under whose shadow to pause were to die. Then huge rocks barred the way.

These were only passed by narrow, winding passages, overhung by the ponderous cliffs above, which ever threatened to fall and engulph the Sojourner. Here the night began to fall; and the dim mist rising from the far-off marshes, took weird shapes of gloom.

In the distant fastnesses of the mountains the wild beasts began to roar in their cavern lairs.

The air became hideous with the fell sounds of the night season. But the poor Poet heeded not ill sights or sounds of dread.

Onwards he went ever-unthinking of the terrors of the night.

To him there was no dread of darkness – no fear of death – no consciousness of horror.

He sought his Beloved One in the Castle of the King; and in that eager quest all natural terrors were forgot. So fared he onwards through the livelong night.

Up the steep defiles he trod.

Through the shadows of the huge rocks he passed unscathed.

The wild animals came around him roaring fiercely – their great eyes flaming like fiery stars through the blackness of the night. From the high rocks great pythons crawled and hung to seize their prey.

From the crevices of the mountain steeps, and from cavernous rifts in the rocky way poisonous serpents glided and rose to strike. But close though the noxious things came, they all refrained to attack; for they knew that the lonely Sojourner was bound for the Castle of their King. Onwards still, onwards he went – unceasing – pausing not in his course – but pressing ever forwards in his quest. When daylight broke at last, the sun rose on a sorry sight.

There, toiling on the rocky way, the poor lonely Poet went ever onwards, unheeding of cold or hunger or pain. His feet were bare, and his footsteps on the rock-strewn way were marked by blood.

Around and behind him, and afar off keeping equal pace on the summits of the rocky ridges, came the wild beasts that looked on him as their prey, but that refrained from touching him because he sought the Castle of their King. In the air wheeled the obscene birds who follow ever on the track of the dying and the lost.

Hovered the bare-necked vultures with eager eyes, and hungry beaks. Their great wings flapped lazily in the idle air as they followed in the Wanderer's track. The vulture are a patient folk, and they await the falling of the prey.

From the cavernous recesses in the black mountain gorges crept, with silent speed, the serpents that there lurk. Came the python, with his colossal folds and endless coils, whence looked forth cunningly the small flat head. Came the boa and all his tribe, which seize their prey by force and crush it with the dread strictness of their embrace. Came the hooded snakes and all those which with their venom destroy their prey. Here, too, came those serpents most terrible of all to their quarry – which fascinate with eyes of weird magic and by the slow gracefulness of their approach. Here came or lay in wait, subtle snakes, which take the colour of herb, or leaf, or dead branch, or slimy pool, amongst which they lurk, and so strike their prey unsuspecting.

Great serpents there were, nimble of body, which hang from rock or branch. These, gripping tight to their distant hold, strike downward with the rapidity of light as they hurl their whip-like bodies from afar upon their prey. Thus came forth all these noxious things to meet the Questing Man, and to assail him.

But when they knew he was bound for the dread Castle of their King, and saw how he went onwards without fear, they abstained from attack. The deadly python and the boa towering aloft, with colossal folds, were passive, and for the nonce, became as stone.

The hooded serpents drew in again their venomous fangs. The mild, deep earnest eyes of the fascinating snake became lurid with baffled spleen, as he felt his power to charm was without avail. In its deadly descent the hanging snake arrested its course, and hung a limp line from rock or branch. Many followed the Wanderer onwards into the desert wilds, waiting and hoping for a chance to destroy. Many other perils also were there for the poor Wanderer in the desert idleness.

As he went onwards the rocky way got steeper and darker.

Lurid fogs and deadly chill mists arose. Then in this path along the trackless wilderness were strange and terrible things. Mandrakes – half plant, half man – shrieked at him with despairing cry, as, helpless for evil, they stretched out their ghastly arms in vain. Giant thorns arose in the path; they pierced his suffering feet and tore his flesh as onwards he trod.

He felt the pain, but he heeded it not. In all the long, terrible journey he had but one idea other than his eager search for his Beloved One.

He thought that the children of men might learn much from the journey towards the Castle of the King, which began so fair, amidst the odorous gardens and under the cool shadow of the spreading trees.

In his heart the Poet spake to the multitude of the children of men; and from his lips the words flowed like music, for he sang of the Golden Gate which the Angels call TRUTH: 'Pass not the Portal of the Sunset Land! Pause where the Angels at their vigil stand.

Be warned! and press not though the gates lie wide, but rest securely on the hither side.

Though odorous gardens and cool ways invite, beyond are darkest valleys of the night.

Rest! Rest contented.

Pause whilst undefiled, Nor seek the horrors of the desert wild.'

Thus treading down all obstacles with his bleeding feet, passed ever onwards, the poor distraught Poet, to seek his Beloved One in the Castle of the King. Even as onwards he went the life that is of the animals seemed to die away behind him.

The jackals and the more cowardly savage animals slunk away.

The lions and tigers, and bears, and wolves, and all the braver of the fierce beasts of prey which followed on his track even after the others had stopped, now began to halt in their career. They growled low and then roared loudly with uplifted heads; the bristles of their mouths quivered with passion, and the great white teeth champed angrily together in baffled rage.

They went on a little further; and stopped again roaring and growling as before.

Then one by one they ceased, and the poor Poet went on alone. In the air the vultures wheeled and screamed, pausing and halting in their flight, as did the savage beasts.

These too ceased at length to follow in air the Wanderer in his onward course. Longest of all kept up the snakes.

With many a writhe and stealthy onward glide, they followed hard upon the footsteps of the Questing Man.

In the blood marks of his feet upon the flinty rocks they found a joy and hope, and they followed ever. But time came when the awful aspect of the places where the Poet passed checked even the serpents in their track – the gloomy defiles whence issue the poisonous winds that sweep with desolation even the dens of the beasts of prey – the sterile fastnesses which march upon the valleys of desolation.

Here even the stealthy serpents paused in their course; and they too fell away. They glided back, smiling with deadliest rancour, to their obscene clefts. Then came places where plants and verdure began to cease. The very weeds became more and more stunted and inane.

Farther on they declined into the sterility of lifeless rock.

Then the most noxious herbs that grew in ghastly shapes of gloom and terror lost even the power to harm, which outlives their living growth.

Dwarfed and stunted even of evil, they were compact of the dead rock.

Here even the deadly Upas tree could strike no root into the pestiferous earth. Then came places where, in the entrance to the Valley of the Shadow, even solid things lost their substance, and melted in the dank and cold mists which swept along. As he passed, the distraught Poet could feel not solid earth under his bleeding feet.

On shadows he walked, and amid them, onwards through the Valley of the Shadow to seek his Beloved One in the Castle of the King. The Valley of the Shadow seemed of endless expanse.

Circled by the teeming mist, no eye could pierce to where rose the great mountains between which the Valley lay. Yet they stood there – Mount Despair on the one hand, and the Hill of Fear upon the other. Hitherto the poor bewildered brain of the Poet had taken no note of all the dangers, and horrors, and pains which surrounded him – save only for the lesson which they taught.

But now, lost as he was in the shrouding vapour of the Valley of the Shadow, he could not but think of the terrors of the way.

He was surrounded by grisly phantoms that ever and anon arose silent in the mist, and were lost again before he could catch to the full their dread import. Then there flashed across his soul a terrible thought: could it be possible that hither his Beloved One had travelled? Had there come to her the pains which shook his own form with agony? Was it indeed necessary that she should have been appalled by all these surrounding horrors? At the thought of her, his Beloved One, suffering such pain and dread, he gave forth one bitter cry that rang through the solitude – that cleft the vapour of the Valley, and echoed in the caverns of the mountains of Despair and Fear. The wild cry prolonged with the agony of the Poet's soul rang through the Valley, till the shadows that peopled it woke for the moment into life-in-death.

They flitted dimly along, now melting away and anon springing again into life – till all the Valley of the Shadow was for once peopled with quickened ghosts. Oh, in that hour there was agony to the poor distraught Poet's soul. But presently there came a calm.

When the rush of his first agony passed, the Poet knew that to the Dead came not the horrors of the journey that he undertook.

To the Quick alone is the horror of the passage to the Castle of the King.

With the thought came to him such peace that even there – in the dark Valley of the Shadow – stole soft music that sounded in the desert gloom like the Music of the Spheres. Then the poor Poet remembered what they had told him; that his Beloved One had walked through the Valley of the Shadow, that she had known the Music of the Spheres, and that she abode in the Castle of the King.

So he thought that as he was now in the Valley of the Shadow, and as he heard the Music of the Spheres, that soon he should see the Castle of the King where his Beloved One abode.

Thus he went on in hope. But alas! that very hope was a new pain that ere this he wot[8] not of. Hitherto he had gone on blindly, recking[9] not of where he went or what came a-nigh him, so long as he pressed onwards on his quest; but now the darkness and the peril of the way had new terrors, for he thought of how they might arrest his course. Such thoughts made the way long indeed, for the moments seemed an age with hoping.

---

[8] to wit *(archaic): to be aware of* (here, *he wot not of: he had no knowledge of*)
[9] to reck *(archaic): to mind or care*

Eagerly he sought for the end to come, when, beyond the Valley of the Shadow through which he fared, he should see rising the turrets of the Castle of the King. Despair seemed to grow upon him; and as it grew there rang out, ever louder, the Music of the Spheres. Onwards, ever onwards, hurried in mad haste the poor distraught Poet.

The dim shadows that peopled the mist shrank back as he passed, extending towards him warning hands with long gloomy fingers of deadly cold.

In the bitter silence of the moment, they seemed to say: 'Go back! Go back!' Louder and louder rang now the Music of the Spheres.

Faster and faster in mad, feverish haste rushed the Poet, amid the shrinking Shadows of the gloomy valley.

The peopling shadows as they faded away before him, seemed to wail in sorrowful warning: 'Go back! Go back!' Still in his ears rang ever the swelling tumult of the music. Faster and faster he rushed onwards; till, at last, wearied nature gave way and he fell prone to earth, senseless, bleeding, and alone. After a time – how long he could not even guess – he awoke from his swoon. For a while he could not think where he was; and his scattered senses could not help him. All was gloom and cold and sadness.

A solitude reigned around him, more deadly than aught[10] he had ever dreamt of.

No breeze was in the air; no movement of a passing cloud.

No voice or stir of living thing in earth, or water, or air.

No rustle of leaf or sway of branch – all was silent, dead, and deserted.

Amid the eternal hills of gloom around lay the valley devoid of aught that lived or grew. The sweeping mists with their multitude of peopling shadows had gone by.

The fearsome terrors of the desert even were not there.

The Poet, as he gazed around him, in his utter loneliness, longed for the sweep of the storm or the roar of the avalanche to break the dread horror of the silent gloom. Then the Poet knew that through the Valley of the Shadow

---

[10] aught *(archaic, literary): anything*

had he come; that scared and maddened though he had been, he had heard the Music of the Spheres.

He thought that now hard by the desolate Kingdom of Death he trod. He gazed all around him, fearing lest he should see anywhere the dread Castle of the King, where his Beloved One abode; and he groaned as the fear of his heart found voice: 'Not here! Oh not here, amid this awful solitude.' Then amid the silence around, upon distant hills his words echoed: 'Not here! Oh not here,' till with the echoing and re-echoing rock, the idle wilderness was peopled with voices. Suddenly the echo voices ceased. From the lurid sky broke the terrible sound of the thunder peal.

Along the distant skies it rolled. Far away over the endless ring of the grey horizon it swept – going and returning – pealing – swelling – dying away.

It traversed the aether, muttering now in ominous sound as of threats, and anon crashing with the voice of dread command. In its roar came a sound as of a word: 'Onwards'. To his knees the Poet sank and welcomed with tears of joy the sound of the thunder.

It swept away as a Power from Above the silent desolation of the wilderness. It told him that in and above the Valley of the Shadow rolled the mighty tones of Heaven's command. Then the Poet rose to his feet, and with new heart went onwards into the wilderness.

As he went the roll of the thunder died away, and again the silence of desolation reigned alone. So time wore on; but never came rest to the weary feet.

Onwards, still onwards he went, with but one memory to cheer him – the echo of the thunder roll in his ears, as it pealed out in the Valley of Desolation: 'Onwards! Onwards!' Now the road became less and less rocky, as on his way he passed.

The great cliffs sank and dwindled away, and the ooze of the fens crept upwards to the mountain's feet. At length the hills and hollows of the mountain fastnesses disappeared.

The Wanderer took his way amid mere trackless wastes, where was nothing but quaking marsh and slime. On, on he wandered; stumbling blindly with weary feet on the endless road. Over his soul crept ever closer the blackness of despair.

Whilst amid the mountain gorges he had been wandering, some small cheer came from the hope that at any moment some turn in the path might show him his journey's end.

Some entry from a dark defile might expose to him, looming great in the distance – or even anigh him – the dread Castle of the King.

But now with the flat desolation of the silent marsh around him, he knew that the Castle could not exist without his seeing it. He stood for awhile erect, and turned him slowly round, so that the complete circuit of the horizon was swept by his eager eyes.

Alas! never a sight did he see.

Nought was there but the black line of the horizon, where the sad earth lay against the level sky.

All, all was compact of a silent gloom. Still on he tottered.

His breath came fast and laboured. His weary limbs quivered as they bore him feebly up.

His strength – his life – was ebbing fast. On, on, he hurried, ever on, with one idea desperately fixed in his poor distraught mind – that in the Castle of the King he should find his Beloved One. He stumbled and fell.

There was no obstacle to arrest his feet; only from his own weakness he declined. Quickly he arose and went onwards with flying feet.

He dreaded that should he fall he might not be able to arise again. Again he fell.

Again he rose and went on his way desperately, with blind purpose. So for a while went he onwards, stumbling and falling; but arising ever and pausing not on his way.

His quest he followed, of his Beloved One abiding in the Castle of the King. At last so weak he grew that when he sank he was unable to rise again. Feebler and feebler he grew as he lay prone; and over his eager eyes came the film of death. But even then came comfort; for he knew that his race was run, and that soon he would meet his Beloved One in the Halls of the Castle of the King. To the wilderness his thoughts he spoke.

His voice came forth with a feeble sound, like the moaning before a storm of the wind as it passes through reeds in the grey autumn:

'A little longer. Soon I shall meet her in the Halls of the

King; and we shall part no more. For this it is worth to pass through the Valley of the Shadow and to listen to the Music of the Spheres with their painful hope.

What boots it though the Castle be afar? Quickly speed the feet of the dead. To the fleeting spirit all distance is but a span. I fear not now to see the Castle of the King; for there, within its chiefest Hall, soon shall I meet my Beloved – to part no more.'

Even as he spoke he felt that the end was nigh. Forth from the marsh before him crept a still, spreading mist.

It rose silently, higher – higher – enveloping the wilderness for far around. It took deeper and darker shades as it arose. It was as though the Spirit of Gloom were hid within, and grew mightier with the spreading vapour.

To the eyes of the dying Poet the creeping mist was as a shadowy castle. Arose the tall turrets and the frowning keep. The gateway with its cavernous recesses and its beetling towers took shape as a skull. The distant battlements towered aloft into the silent air. From the very ground whereon the stricken Poet lay, grew, dim and dark, a vast causeway leading into the gloom of the Castle gate.

The dying Poet raised his head and looked.

His fast failing eyes, quickened by the love and hope of his spirit, pierced through the dark walls of the keep and the gloomy terrors of the gateway. There, within the great Hall where the grim King of Terrors himself holds his court, he saw her whom he sought.

She was standing in the ranks of those who wait in patience for their Beloved to follow them into the Land of Death. The Poet knew that he had but a little while to wait, and he was patient – stricken though he lay, amongst the Eternal Solitudes. Afar off, beyond the distant horizon, came a faint light as of the dawn of a coming day. As it grew brighter the Castle stood out more and more clearly; till in the quickening dawn it stood revealed in all its cold expanse. The dying Poet knew that the end was at hand.

With a last effort he raised himself to his feet, that standing erect and bold, as is the right of manhood, he might so meet face to face the grim King of Death before the eyes of his Beloved One. The distant sun of the coming day rose over the horizon's edge. A ray of light shot upwards. As it struck the summit of the Castle keep the Poet's Spirit in an instant of time swept along the causeway.

Through the ghostly portal of the Castle it swept, and met with joy the kindred Spirit that it loved before the very face of the King of Death. Quicker then than the lightning's flash the whole Castle melted into nothingness; and the sun of the coming day shone calmly down upon the Eternal Solitudes. In the Land within the Portal rose the sun of the coming day.

It shone calmly and brightly on a fair garden, where, among the long summer grass lay the Poet, colder than the marble statues around him.

DRACULA'S GUEST

When we started for our drive the sun was shining brightly on Munich, and the air was full of the joyousness of early summer. Just as we were about to depart, Herr Delbrück (the maître d'hôtel of the Quatre Saisons, where I was staying) came down, bareheaded, to the carriage and, after wishing me a pleasant drive, said to the coachman, still holding his hand on the handle of the carriage door:

'Remember you are back by nightfall. The sky looks bright but there is a shiver in the north wind that says there may be a sudden storm. But I am sure you will not be late.' Here he smiled, and added, 'for you know what night it is.'

Johann answered with an emphatic, 'Ja, mein Herr[1],' and, touching his hat, drove off quickly. When we had cleared the town, I said, after signalling to him to stop: 'Tell me, Johann, what is tonight?'

He crossed himself, as he answered laconically: 'Walpurgis Nacht[2].' Then he took out his watch, a great, old-fashioned German silver thing as big as a turnip, and looked at it, with his eyebrows gathered together and a little impatient shrug of his shoulders. I realised that this was his way of respectfully protesting against the unnecessary delay, and sank back in the carriage, merely motioning him to proceed. He started off rapidly, as if to make up for lost time. Every now and then the horses seemed to throw up their heads and sniffed the air suspiciously. On such occasions I often looked round in alarm. The road was pretty bleak, for we were traversing a sort of high, wind-swept plateau. As we drove, I saw a road that looked but little used, and which seemed to dip through a little, winding valley. It looked so inviting that, even at the risk of offending him, I called Johann to stop – and when he had pulled up, I told him I would like to drive down that road. He made all sorts of excuses, and frequently crossed himself as he spoke. This somewhat piqued my curiosity, so I asked him various

---

[1] Ja, mein Herr: *(German) Yes, sir*
[2] Walpurgis Nacht: *Walpurgis Night, the eve of May 1st, one of the feast days of St Walpurga, an eighth-century English missionary to the Frankish empire. In German folklore, this was believed to be the night on which witches would meet in the Harz Mountains*

questions. He answered fencingly, and repeatedly looked at his watch in protest. Finally I said:

'Well, Johann, I want to go down this road. I shall not ask you to come unless you like; but tell me why you do not like to go, that is all I ask.'

For answer he seemed to throw himself off the box, so quickly did he reach the ground. Then he stretched out his hands appealingly to me, and implored me not to go. There was just enough of English mixed with the German for me to understand the drift of his talk. He seemed always just about to tell me something – the very idea of which evidently frightened him; but each time he pulled himself up, saying, as he crossed himself: 'Walpurgis Nacht!'

I tried to argue with him, but it was difficult to argue with a man when I did not know his language. The advantage certainly rested with him, for although he began to speak in English, of a very crude and broken kind, he always got excited and broke into his native tongue – and every time he did so, he looked at his watch. Then the horses became restless and sniffed the air. At this he grew very pale, and, looking around in a frightened way, he suddenly jumped forwards, took them by the bridles and led them on some twenty feet. I followed, and asked why he had done this. For answer he crossed himself, pointed to the spot we had left and drew his carriage in the direction of the other road, indicating a cross, and said, first in German, then in English: 'Buried him – him what killed themselves.'

I remembered the old custom of burying suicides at crossroads: 'Ah! I see, a suicide. How interesting!' But for the life of me I could not make out why the horses were frightened.

Whilst we were talking, we heard a sort of sound between a yelp and a bark. It was far away; but the horses got very restless, and it took Johann all his time to quiet them. He was pale, and said, 'It sounds like a wolf – but yet there are no wolves here now.'

'No?' I said, questioning him; 'isn't it long since the wolves were so near the city?'

'Long, long,' he answered, 'in the spring and summer; but with the snow the wolves have been here not so long.'

Whilst he was petting the horses and trying to quiet them, dark clouds drifted rapidly across the sky. The sunshine passed away, and a breath of cold wind seemed to drift past us. It was only a breath, however, and more in the nature of a warning than a fact, for the sun came out brightly again. Johann looked under his lifted hand at the horizon and said: 'The storm of snow, he comes before long time.' Then he looked at his watch again, and, straightway holding his reins firmly – for the horses were still pawing the ground restlessly and shaking their heads – he climbed to his box as though the time had come for proceeding on our journey.

I felt a little obstinate and did not at once get into the carriage.

'Tell me,' I said, 'about this place where the road leads,' and I pointed down.

Again he crossed himself and mumbled a prayer, before he answered, 'It is unholy.'

'What is unholy?' I enquired.

'The village.'

'Then there is a village?'

'No, no. No one lives there hundreds of years.'

My curiosity was piqued, 'But you said there was a village.'

'There was.'

'Where is it now?'

Whereupon he burst out into a long story in German and English, so mixed up that I could not quite understand exactly what he said, but roughly I gathered that long ago, hundreds of years, men had died there and been buried in their graves; and sounds were heard under the clay, and when the graves were opened, men and women were found rosy with life, and their mouths red with blood. And so, in haste to save their lives (aye, and their souls! – and here he crossed himself) those who were left fled away to other places, where the living lived, and the dead were dead and not – not something. He was evidently afraid to speak the last words. As he proceeded with his narration, he grew more and more excited. It seemed as if his imagination had got hold of him, and he ended in a perfect paroxysm of fear – white-faced, perspiring, trembling and looking round him, as if expecting that some dreadful presence would manifest itself there in the bright sunshine on the open plain. Finally, in an agony of desperation, he cried: 'Walpurgis Nacht!' and pointed to the carriage for me to get in. All my English blood rose at this, and, standing back, I said: 'You are afraid, Johann – you are afraid. Go home; I shall return alone; the walk will do me good.'

The carriage door was open. I took from the seat my oak walking-stick – which I always carry on my holiday excursions – and closed the door, pointing back to Munich, and said, 'Go home, Johann – Walpurgis Nacht doesn't concern Englishmen.'

The horses were now more restive than ever, and Johann was trying to hold them in, while excitedly imploring me not to do anything so foolish. I pitied the poor fellow, he was deeply in earnest; but all the same I could not help laughing. His English was quite gone now. In his anxiety he had forgotten that his only means of making me understand was to talk my language, so he jabbered away in his native German. It began to be a little tedious. After giving the direction, 'Home!' I turned to go down the cross-road into the valley.

With a despairing gesture, Johann turned his horses towards Munich. I leaned on my stick and looked after him. He went slowly along the road for a while: then there came over the crest of the hill a man tall and thin. I could see so much in the distance. When he drew near the horses, they began to jump and kick about, then to scream with terror. Johann could not hold them in; they bolted down the road, running away madly. I watched them out of sight, then looked for the stranger, but I found that he, too, was gone.

With a light heart I turned down the side road through the deepening valley to which Johann had objected. There was not the slightest reason, that I could see, for his objection; and I daresay I tramped for a couple of hours without thinking of time or distance, and certainly without seeing a person or a house. So far as the place was concerned, it was desolation, itself. But I did not notice this particularly till, on turning a bend in the road, I came upon a scattered fringe of wood; then I recognised that I had been impressed unconsciously by the desolation of the region through which I had passed.

I sat down to rest myself, and began to look around. It struck me that it was considerably colder than it had been at the commencement of my walk – a sort of sighing sound seemed to be around me, with, now and then, high overhead, a sort of muffled roar. Looking upwards I noticed that great thick clouds were drifting rapidly across the sky from north to south at a great height. There were signs of coming storm in some lofty stratum of the air. I was a little chilly, and, thinking that it was the sitting still after the exercise of walking, I resumed my journey.

The ground I passed over was now much more picturesque. There were no striking objects that the eye might single out; but in all there was a charm of beauty. I took little heed of time and it was only when the deepening twilight forced itself upon me that I began to think of how I should find my way home. The brightness of the day had gone. The air was cold, and the drifting of clouds high overhead was more marked. They were accompanied by a sort of faraway rushing sound, through which seemed to come at intervals that mysterious cry which the driver had said came from a wolf. For a while I hesitated. I had said I would see the deserted village, so on I went, and presently came on a wide stretch of open country, shut in by hills all around. Their sides were covered with trees which spread down to the plain, dotting, in clumps, the gentler slopes and hollows which showed here and there. I followed with my eye the winding of the road, and saw that it curved close to one of the densest of these clumps and was lost behind it.

As I looked there came a cold shiver in the air, and the snow began to fall. I thought of the miles and miles of bleak country I had passed, and then hurried on to seek the shelter of the wood in front. Darker and darker grew the sky, and faster and heavier fell the snow, till the earth before and around me was a glistening white carpet the further edge of which was lost in misty vagueness. The road was here but crude, and when on the level its boundaries were not so marked, as when it passed through the cuttings; and in a little while I found that I must have strayed from it, for I missed underfoot the hard surface, and my feet sank deeper in the grass and moss. Then the wind grew stronger and blew with ever increasing force, till I was fain to run before it. The air became icy-cold, and in spite of my exercise I began to suffer. The snow was now falling so thickly and whirling around me in such rapid eddies that I could hardly keep my eyes open.

Every now and then the heavens were torn asunder by vivid lightning, and in the flashes I could see ahead of me a great mass of trees, chiefly yew and cypress all heavily coated with snow.

I was soon amongst the shelter of the trees, and there, in comparative silence, I could hear the rush of the wind high overhead. Presently the blackness of the storm had become merged in the darkness of the night. By and by the storm seemed to be passing away: it now only came in fierce puffs or blasts. At such moments the weird sound of the wolf appeared to be echoed by many similar sounds around me.

Now and again, through the black mass of drifting cloud, came a straggling ray of moonlight, which lit up the expanse, and showed me that I was at the edge of a dense mass of cypress and yew trees. As the snow had ceased to fall, I walked out from the shelter and began to investigate more closely. It appeared to me that, amongst so many old foundations as I had passed, there might be still standing a house in which, though in ruins, I could find some sort of shelter for a while. As I skirted the edge of the copse, I found that a low wall encircled it, and following this I presently found an opening. Here the cypresses formed an alley leading up to a square mass of some kind of building. Just as I caught sight of this, however, the drifting clouds obscured the moon, and I passed up the path in darkness. The wind must have grown colder, for I felt myself shiver as I walked; but there was hope of shelter, and I groped my way blindly on.

I stopped, for there was a sudden stillness. The storm had passed; and, perhaps in sympathy with nature's silence, my heart seemed to cease to beat. But this was only momentarily; for suddenly the moonlight broke through the clouds, showing me that I was in a graveyard, and that the square object before me was a great massive tomb of marble, as white as the snow that lay on and all around it. With the moonlight there came a fierce sigh of the storm, which appeared to resume its course with a long, low howl, as of many dogs or wolves. I was awed and shocked, and felt the cold perceptibly grow upon me till it seemed to grip me by the heart. Then while the flood of moonlight still fell on the marble tomb, the storm gave further evidence of renewing, as though it was returning on its track. Impelled by some sort of fascination, I approached the sepulchre to see what it was, and why such a thing stood alone in such a place. I walked around it, and read, over the Doric door, in German:

COUNTESS DOLINGEN OF GRATZ
IN STYRIA
SOUGHT AND FOUND DEATH
1801

On the top of the tomb, seemingly driven through the solid marble – for the structure was composed of a few vast blocks of stone – was a great iron spike or stake. On going to the back I saw, graven in great Russian letters:

'The dead travel fast.'

There was something so weird and uncanny about the whole thing that it gave me a turn and made me feel quite faint. I began to wish, for the first time, that I had taken Johann's advice. Here a thought struck me, which came under almost mysterious circumstances and with a terrible shock. This was Walpurgis Night!

Walpurgis Night, when, according to the belief of millions of people, the devil was abroad – when the graves were opened and the dead came forth and walked. When all evil things of earth and air and water held revel. This very place the driver had specially shunned. This was the depopulated village of centuries ago. This was where the suicide lay; and this was the place where I was alone – unmanned, shivering with cold in a shroud of snow with a wild storm gathering again upon me! It took all my philosophy, all the religion I had been taught, all my courage, not to collapse in a paroxysm of fright.

And now a perfect tornado burst upon me. The ground shook as though thousands of horses thundered across it; and this time the storm bore on its icy wings, not snow, but great hailstones which drove with such violence that they might have come from the thongs of Balearic slingers[3] – hailstones that beat down leaf and branch and made the shelter of the

---

[3] Balearic slingers: *members of the Carthaginian mercenary army renowned for their ability to kill their opponents at great distance simply using a leather sling and a stone*

cypresses of no more avail than though their stems were standing corn. At the first I had rushed to the nearest tree; but I was soon fain to leave it and seek the only spot that seemed to afford refuge, the deep Doric doorway of the marble tomb. There, crouching against the massive bronze door, I gained a certain amount of protection from the beating of the hailstones, for now they only drove against me as they ricocheted from the ground and the side of the marble.

As I leaned against the door, it moved slightly and opened inwards. The shelter of even a tomb was welcome in that pitiless tempest, and I was about to enter it when there came a flash of forked-lightning that lit up the whole expanse of the heavens. In the instant, as I am a living man, I saw, as my eyes were turned into the darkness of the tomb, a beautiful woman, with rounded cheeks and red lips, seemingly sleeping on a bier. As the thunder broke overhead, I was grasped as by the hand of a giant and hurled out into the storm. The whole thing was so sudden that, before I could realise the shock, moral as well as physical, I found the hailstones beating me down. At the same time I had a strange, dominating feeling that I was not alone. I looked towards the tomb. Just then there came another blinding flash, which seemed to strike the iron stake that surmounted the tomb and to pour through to the earth, blasting and crumbling the marble, as in a burst of flame. The dead woman rose for a moment of agony, while she was lapped in the flame, and her bitter scream of pain was drowned in the thundercrash. The last thing I heard was this mingling of dreadful sound, as again I was seized in the giant-grasp and dragged away, while the hailstones beat on me, and the air around seemed reverberant with the howling of wolves. The last sight that I remembered was a vague, white, moving mass, as if all the graves around me had sent out the phantoms of their sheeted-dead, and that they were closing in on me through the white cloudiness of the driving hail.

Gradually there came a sort of vague beginning of consciousness; then a sense of weariness that was dreadful. For a time I remembered nothing; but slowly my senses returned. My feet seemed positively racked with pain, yet I could not move them. They seemed to be numbed. There was an icy feeling at the back of my neck and all down my spine, and my ears, like my feet, were dead, yet in torment; but there was in my breast a sense of warmth which was, by comparison, delicious. It was as a nightmare – a physical nightmare, if one may use such an expression; for some heavy weight on my chest made it difficult for me to breathe.

This period of semi-lethargy seemed to remain a long time, and as it faded away I must have slept or swooned. Then came a sort of loathing, like the first stage of sea-sickness, and a wild desire to be free from something – I knew not what. A vast stillness enveloped me, as though all the world were asleep or dead – only broken by the low panting as of some animal close to me. I felt a warm rasping at my throat, then came a consciousness of the awful truth, which chilled me to the heart and sent the blood surging up through my brain. Some great animal was lying on me and now licking my throat. I feared to stir, for some instinct of prudence bade me lie still; but the brute seemed to realise that there was now some change in me, for it raised its head. Through my eyelashes I saw above me the two great flaming eyes of a gigantic wolf. Its sharp white teeth gleamed in the gaping red mouth, and I could feel its hot breath, fierce and acrid, upon me.

For another spell of time I remembered no more. Then I became conscious of a low growl, followed by a yelp, renewed again and again. Then, seemingly very far away, I heard a 'Holloa! holloa!' as of many voices calling in unison. Cautiously I raised my head and looked in the direction whence the sound came; but the cemetery blocked my view. The wolf still continued to yelp in a strange way, and a red glare began to move round the grove of cypresses, as though following the sound. As the voices drew closer, the wolf yelped faster and louder. I feared to make either sound or motion. Nearer came the red glow, over the white pall which stretched into the darkness around me. Then all at once from beyond the trees there came at a trot a troop of horsemen bearing torches. The wolf rose from my breast and made for the cemetery. I saw one of the horsemen (soldiers by their caps and their long military cloaks) raise his carbine and take aim. A companion knocked up his arm, and I heard the ball whizz over my head. He had evidently taken my body for that of the wolf. Another sighted the animal as it slunk away, and a shot followed. Then, at a gallop, the troop rode forwards – some towards me, others following the wolf as it disappeared amongst the snow-clad cypresses.

As they drew nearer I tried to move, but was powerless, although I could see and hear all that went on around me. Two or three of the soldiers jumped from their horses and knelt beside me. One of them raised my head, and placed his hand over my heart.

'Good news, comrades!' he cried. 'His heart still beats!'

Then some brandy was poured down my throat; it put vigour into me, and I was able to open my eyes fully and look around. Lights and shadows were moving among the trees, and I heard men call to one another. They drew together, uttering frightened exclamations; and the lights flashed as the others came pouring out of the cemetery pell-mell, like men possessed. When the further ones came close to us, those who were around me asked them eagerly:

'Well, have you found him?'

The reply rang out hurriedly:

'No! no! Come away quick – quick! This is no place to stay, and on this of all nights!'

'What was it?' was the question, asked in all manner of keys. The answer came variously and all indefinitely as though the men were moved by some common impulse to speak, yet were restrained by some common fear from giving their thoughts.

'It – it – indeed!' gibbered one, whose wits had plainly given out for the moment.

'A wolf – and yet not a wolf!' another put in shudderingly.

'No use trying for him without the sacred bullet,' a third remarked in a more ordinary manner.

'Serve us right for coming out on this night! Truly we have earned our thousand marks!' were the ejaculations of a fourth.

'There was blood on the broken marble,' another said after a pause – 'the lightning never brought that there. And for him – is he safe? Look at his throat! See, comrades, the wolf has been lying on him and keeping his blood warm.'

The officer looked at my throat and replied:

'He is all right; the skin is not pierced. What does it all mean? We should never have found him but for the yelping of the wolf.'

'What became of it?' asked the man who was holding up my head, and who seemed the least panic-stricken of the party, for his hands were steady and without tremor. On his sleeve was the chevron of a petty officer.

'It went to its home,' answered the man, whose long face was pallid, and who actually shook with terror as he glanced around him fearfully. 'There are graves enough there in which it may lie. Come, comrades – come quickly! Let us leave this cursed spot.'

The officer raised me to a sitting posture, as he uttered a word of command; then several men placed me upon a horse. He sprang to the saddle behind me, took me in his arms, gave the word to advance; and, turning our faces away from the cypresses, we rode away in swift, military order.

As yet my tongue refused its office, and I was perforce silent. I must have fallen asleep; for the next thing I remembered was finding myself standing up, supported by a soldier on each side of me. It was almost broad daylight, and to the north a red streak of sunlight was reflected, like a path of blood, over the waste of snow. The officer was telling the men to say nothing of what they had seen, except that they found an English stranger, guarded by a large dog.

'Dog! that was no dog,' cut in the man who had exhibited such fear. 'I think I know a wolf when I see one.'

The young officer answered calmly: 'I said a dog.'

'Dog!' reiterated the other ironically. It was evident that his courage was rising with the sun; and, pointing to me, he said, 'Look at his throat. Is that the work of a dog, master?'

Instinctively I raised my hand to my throat, and as I touched it I cried out in pain. The men crowded round to look, some stooping down from their saddles; and again there came the calm voice of the young officer: 'A dog, as I said. If aught else were said we should only be laughed at.'

I was then mounted behind a trooper, and we rode on into the suburbs of Munich. Here we came across a stray carriage, into which I was lifted, and it was driven off to the Quatre Saisons – the young officer accompanying me, whilst a trooper followed with his horse, and the others rode off to their barracks.

When we arrived, Herr Delbrück rushed so quickly down the steps to meet me, that it was apparent he had been watching within. Taking me by both hands he solicitously led me in. The officer saluted me and was turning to withdraw, when I recognised his purpose, and insisted that he should come to my rooms. Over a glass of wine I warmly thanked him and his brave comrades for saving me. He replied simply that he was more than glad, and that Herr Delbrück had at the first taken steps to make all the searching party pleased; at which ambiguous utterance the maître d'hôtel smiled, while the officer pleaded duty and withdrew.

'But Herr Delbrück,' I enquired, 'how and why was it that the soldiers searched for me?'

He shrugged his shoulders, as if in depreciation of his own deed, as he replied:

'I was so fortunate as to obtain leave from the commander of the regiment in which I served, to ask for volunteers.'

'But how did you know I was lost?' I asked.

'The driver came hither with the remains of his carriage, which had been upset when the horses ran away.'

'But surely you would not send a search-party of soldiers merely on this account?'

'Oh, no!' he answered; 'but even before the coachman arrived, I had this telegram from the Boyar[4] whose guest you are,' and he took from his pocket a telegram which he handed to me, and I read:

> Bistritz.
> Be careful of my guest – his safety is most precious to me. Should aught happen to him, or if he be missed, spare nothing to find him and ensure his safety. He is English and therefore adventurous. There are often dangers from snow and wolves and night. Lose not a moment if you suspect harm to him. I answer your zeal with my fortune.
>
> – Dracula.

As I held the telegram in my hand, the room seemed to whirl around me; and, if the attentive maître d'hôtel had not caught me, I think I should have fallen. There was something so strange in all this, something so weird and impossible to

---

[4] Boyar: *member of an old order of the Russian aristocracy*

imagine, that there grew on me a sense of my being in some way the sport of opposite forces – the mere vague idea of which seemed in a way to paralyse me. I was certainly under some form of mysterious protection. From a distant country had come, in the very nick of time, a message that took me out of the danger of the snow-sleep and the jaws of the wolf.

THE SECRET OF THE GROWING GOLD

When Margaret Delandre went to live at Brent's Rock the whole neighbourhood awoke to the pleasure of an entirely new scandal.

Scandals in connection with either the Delandre family or the Brents of Brent's Rock, were not few; and if the secret history of the county had been written in full both names would have been found well represented.

It is true that the status of each was so different that they might have belonged to different continents – or to different worlds for the matter of that – for hitherto their orbits had never crossed.

The Brents were accorded by the whole section of the country a unique social dominance, and had ever held themselves as high above the yeoman[1] class to which Margaret Delandre belonged, as a blue-blooded Spanish hidalgo out-tops his peasant tenantry.

The Delandres had an ancient record and were proud of it in their way as the Brents were of theirs.

But the family had never risen above yeomanry; and although they had been once well-to-do in the good old times of foreign wars and protection, their fortunes had withered under the scorching of the free trade sun and the 'piping times of peace.' They had, as the elder members used to assert, 'stuck to the land', with the result that they had taken root in it, body and soul.

In fact, they, having chosen the life of vegetables, had flourished as vegetation does – blossomed and thrived in the good season and suffered in the bad.

Their holding, Dander's Croft, seemed to have been worked out, and to be typical of the family which had inhabited it.

The latter had declined generation after generation, sending out now and again some abortive shoot of unsatisfied energy in the shape of a soldier or sailor, who had worked his way to the minor grades of the services and had there stopped, cut short either from unheeding gallantry in action or from that destroying cause to men

[1] yeoman: *(historical) a small landowner living off his own land*

without breeding or youthful care – the recognition of a position above them which they feel unfitted to fill.

So, little by little, the family dropped lower and lower, the men brooding and dissatisfied, and drinking themselves into the grave, the women drudging at home, or marrying beneath them – or worse.

In process of time all disappeared, leaving only two in the Croft, Wykham Delandre and his sister Margaret.

The man and woman seemed to have inherited in masculine and feminine form respectively the evil tendency of their race, sharing in common the principles, though manifesting them in different ways, of sullen passion, voluptuousness and recklessness.

The history of the Brents had been something similar, but showing the causes of decadence in their aristocratic and not their plebeian forms.

They, too, had sent their shoots to the wars; but their positions had been different and they had often attained honour – for without flaw they were gallant, and brave deeds were done by them before the selfish dissipation which marked them had sapped their vigour.

The present head of the family – if family it could now be called when one remained of the direct line – was Geoffrey Brent.

He was almost a type of worn out race, manifesting in some ways its most brilliant qualities, and in others its utter degradation.

He might be fairly compared with some of those antique Italian nobles whom the painters have preserved to us with their courage, their unscrupulousness, their refinement of lust and cruelty – the voluptuary actual with the fiend potential.

He was certainly handsome, with that dark, aquiline, commanding beauty which women so generally recognise as dominant.

With men he was distant and cold; but such a bearing never deters womankind.

The inscrutable laws of sex have so arranged that even a timid woman is not afraid of a fierce and haughty man.

And so it was that there was hardly a woman of any kind or degree, who lived within view of Brent's Rock, who did not cherish some form of secret admiration for the handsome wastrel.

The category was a wide one, for Brent's Rock rose up steeply from the midst of a level region and for a circuit of a hundred miles it lay on the horizon, with its high old towers and steep roofs cutting the level edge of wood and hamlet, and far-scattered mansions.

So long as Geoffrey Brent confined his dissipations to London and Paris and Vienna – anywhere out of sight and sound of his home – opinion was silent.

It is easy to listen to far-off echoes unmoved, and we can treat them with disbelief, or scorn, or disdain, or whatever attitude of coldness may suit our purpose.

But when the scandal came close home it was another matter; and the feeling of independence and integrity which is in people of every community which is not utterly spoiled, asserted itself and demanded that condemnation should be expressed.

Still there was a certain reticence in all, and no more notice was taken of the existing facts than was absolutely necessary.

Margaret Delandre bore herself so fearlessly and so openly – she accepted her position as the justified companion of Geoffrey Brent so naturally that people came to believe that she was secretly married to him, and therefore thought it wiser to hold their tongues lest[2] time should justify her and also make her an active enemy.

The one person who, by his interference, could have settled all doubts was debarred by circumstances from interfering in the matter. Wykham Delandre had quarrelled with his sister – or perhaps it was that she had quarrelled with him – and they were on terms not merely of armed neutrality but of bitter hatred.

The quarrel had been antecedent to Margaret going to Brent's Rock. She and Wykham had almost come to blows. There had certainly been threats on one side and on the other; and in the end Wykham, overcome with passion, had ordered his sister to leave his house. She had risen straightway, and, without waiting to pack up even her own personal belongings, had walked out of the house.

---

[2] lest: *(archaic) for fear that*

On the threshold she had paused for a moment to hurl a bitter threat at Wykham that he would rue in shame and despair to the last hour of his life his act of that day.

Some weeks had since passed; and it was understood in the neighbourhood that Margaret had gone to London, when she suddenly appeared driving out with Geoffrey Brent, and the entire neighbourhood knew before nightfall that she had taken up her abode at the Rock.

It was no subject of surprise that Brent had come back unexpectedly, for such was his usual custom. Even his own servants never knew when to expect him, for there was a private door, of which he alone had the key, by which he sometimes entered without anyone in the house being aware of his coming.

This was his usual method of appearing after a long absence. Wykham Delandre was furious at the news.

He vowed vengeance – and to keep his mind level with his passion drank deeper than ever. He tried several times to see his sister, but she contemptuously refused to meet him. He tried to have an interview with Brent and was refused by him also. Then he tried to stop him in the road, but without avail, for Geoffrey was not a man to be stopped against his will.

Several actual encounters took place between the two men, and many more were threatened and avoided. At last Wykham Delandre settled down to a morose, vengeful acceptance of the situation.

Neither Margaret nor Geoffrey was of a pacific temperament, and it was not long before there began to be quarrels between them. One thing would lead to another, and wine flowed freely at Brent's Rock.

Now and again the quarrels would assume a bitter aspect, and threats would be exchanged in uncompromising language that fairly awed the listening servants.

But such quarrels generally ended where domestic altercations do, in reconciliation, and in a mutual respect for the fighting qualities proportionate to their manifestation.

Fighting for its own sake is found by a certain class of persons, all the world over, to be a matter of absorbing interest, and there is no reason to believe that domestic conditions minimise its potency.

Geoffrey and Margaret made occasional absences from Brent's Rock, and on each of these occasions Wykham Delandre also absented himself; but as he generally heard of the absence too late to be of any service, he returned home each time in a more bitter and discontented frame of mind than before.

At last there came a time when the absence from Brent's Rock became longer than before. Only a few days earlier there had been a quarrel, exceeding in bitterness anything which had gone before; but this, too, had been made up, and a trip on the Continent had been mentioned before the servants.

After a few days Wykham Delandre also went away, and it was some weeks before he returned.

It was noticed that he was full of some new importance – satisfaction, exaltation – they hardly knew how to call it.

He went straightway to Brent's Rock, and demanded to see Geoffrey Brent, and on being told that he had not yet returned, said, with a grim decision which the servants noted: 'I shall come again. My news is solid – it can wait!' and turned away.

Week after week went by, and month after month; and then there came a rumour, certified later on, that an accident had occurred in the Zermatt[3] valley.

Whilst crossing a dangerous pass the carriage containing an English lady and the driver had fallen over a precipice, the gentleman of the party, Mr Geoffrey Brent, having been fortunately saved as he had been walking up the hill to ease the horses. He gave information, and search was made. The broken rail, the excoriated roadway, the marks where the horses had struggled on the decline before finally pitching over into the torrent – all told the sad tale.

It was a wet season, and there had been much snow in the winter, so that the river was swollen beyond its usual volume, and the eddies of the stream were packed with ice.

All search was made, and finally the wreck of the carriage and the body of one horse were found in an eddy of the river. Later on the body of the driver was found on the sandy, torrent-swept waste near Taesch; but the body of the lady, like that of the other horse, had quite disappeared, and

[3] Zermatt: *a small resort in the canton of Valais in southern Switzerland*

was – what was left of it by that time – whirling amongst the eddies of the Rhône on its way down to the Lake of Geneva.

Wykham Delandre made all the enquiries possible, but could not find any trace of the missing woman.

He found, however, in the books of the various hotels the name of 'Mr and Mrs Geoffrey Brent'.

And he had a stone erected at Zermatt to his sister's memory, under her married name, and a tablet put up in the church at Bretten, the parish in which both Brent's Rock and Dander's Croft were situated.

There was a lapse of nearly a year, after the excitement of the matter had worn away, and the whole neighbourhood had gone on its accustomed way.

Brent was still absent, and Delandre more drunken, more morose, and more revengeful than before.

Then there was a new excitement.

Brent's Rock was being made ready for a new mistress.

It was officially announced by Geoffrey himself in a letter to the vicar, that he had been married some months before to an Italian lady, and that they were then on their way home.

Then a small army of workmen invaded the house; and hammer and plane sounded, and a general air of size and paint pervaded the atmosphere.

One wing of the old house, the south, was entirely re-done; and then the great body of the workmen departed, leaving only materials for the doing of the old hall when Geoffrey Brent should have returned, for he had directed that the decoration was only to be done under his own eyes.

He had brought with him accurate drawings of a hall in the house of his bride's father, for he wished to reproduce for her the place to which she had been accustomed.

As the moulding had all to be re-done, some scaffolding poles and boards were brought in and laid on one side of the great hall, and also a great wooden tank or box for mixing the lime, which was laid in bags beside it.

When the new mistress of Brent's Rock arrived the bells of the church rang out, and there was a general jubilation.

She was a beautiful creature, full of the poetry and fire and passion of the South; and the few English words which she had learned were spoken in such a sweet and pretty broken way that she won the hearts of the people almost as much by the music of her voice as by the melting beauty of her dark eyes.

Geoffrey Brent seemed more happy than he had ever before appeared; but there was a dark, anxious look on his face that was new to those who knew him of old, and he started at times as though at some noise that was unheard by others.

And so months passed and the whisper grew that at last Brent's Rock was to have an heir. Geoffrey was very tender to his wife, and the new bond between them seemed to soften him. He took more interest in his tenants and their needs than he had ever done; and works of charity on his part as well as on his sweet young wife's were not lacking.

He seemed to have set all his hopes on the child that was coming, and as he looked deeper into the future the dark shadow that had come over his face seemed to die gradually away.

All the time Wykham Delandre nursed his revenge. Deep in his heart had grown up a purpose of vengeance which only waited an opportunity to crystallise and take a definite shape.

His vague idea was somehow centred in the wife of Brent, for he knew that he could strike him best through those he loved, and the coming time seemed to hold in its womb the opportunity for which he longed.

One night he sat alone in the living room of his house. It had once been a handsome room in its way, but time and neglect had done their work and it was now little better than a ruin, without dignity or picturesqueness of any kind.

He had been drinking heavily for some time and was more than half stupefied. He thought he heard a noise as of someone at the door and looked up. Then he called half savagely to come in; but there was no response. With a muttered blasphemy he renewed his potations.

Presently he forgot all around him, sank into a daze, but suddenly awoke to see standing before him someone or something like a battered, ghostly edition of his sister.

For a few moments there came upon him a sort of fear.

The woman before him, with distorted features and burning eyes seemed hardly human, and the only thing that seemed a reality of his sister, as she had been, was her wealth of golden hair, and this was now streaked with grey.

She eyed her brother with a long, cold stare; and he, too, as he looked and began to realise the actuality of her presence, found the hatred of her which he had had, once again surging up in his heart.

All the brooding passion of the past year seemed to find a voice at once as he asked her: 'Why are you here? You're dead and buried.'

'I am here, Wykham Delandre, for no love of you, but because I hate another even more than I do you!' A great passion blazed in her eyes.

'Him?' he asked, in so fierce a whisper that even the woman was for an instant startled till she regained her calm.

'Yes, him!' she answered. 'But make no mistake, my revenge is my own; and I merely use you to help me to it.'

Wykham asked suddenly: 'Did he marry you?'

The woman's distorted face broadened out in a ghastly attempt at a smile.

It was a hideous mockery, for the broken features and seamed scars took strange shapes and strange colours, and queer lines of white showed out as the straining muscles pressed on the old cicatrices.

'So you would like to know! It would please your pride to feel that your sister was truly married! Well, you shall not know. That was my revenge on you, and I do not mean to change it by a hair's breadth. I have come here tonight simply to let you know that I am alive, so that if any violence be done me where I am going there may be a witness.'

'Where are you going?' demanded her brother.

'That is my affair! and I have not the least intention of letting you know!'

Wykham stood up, but the drink was on him and he reeled and fell.

As he lay on the floor he announced his intention of following his sister; and with an outburst of splenetic humour told her that he would follow her through the darkness by the light of her hair, and of her beauty.

At this she turned on him, and said that there were others beside him that would rue her hair and her beauty too.

'As he will,' she hissed; 'for the hair remains though the

beauty be gone. When he withdrew the lynch-pin[4] and sent us over the precipice into the torrent, he had little thought of my beauty. Perhaps his beauty would be scarred like mine were he whirled, as I was, among the rocks of the Visp[5], and frozen on the ice pack in the drift of the river. But let him beware! His time is coming!' and with a fierce gesture she flung open the door and passed out into the night.

* * * * *

Later on that night, Mrs Brent, who was but half-asleep, became suddenly awake and spoke to her husband: 'Geoffrey, was not that the click of a lock somewhere below our window?' But Geoffrey – though she thought that he, too, had started at the noise – seemed sound asleep, and breathed heavily.

Again Mrs Brent dozed; but this time awoke to the fact that her husband had arisen and was partially dressed.

He was deadly pale, and when the light of the lamp which he had in his hand fell on his face, she was frightened at the look in his eyes.

'What is it, Geoffrey? What dost thou?[6]' she asked.

'Hush! little one,' he answered, in a strange, hoarse voice. 'Go to sleep. I am restless, and wish to finish some work I left undone.

'Bring it here, my husband,' she said; 'I am lonely and I fear when thou art[7] away.' For reply he merely kissed her and went out, closing the door behind him.

She lay awake for awhile, and then nature asserted itself, and she slept.

Suddenly she started broad awake with the memory in her ears of a smothered cry from somewhere not far off.

She jumped up and ran to the door and listened, but there was no sound. She grew alarmed for her husband, and called out: 'Geoffrey! Geoffrey!' After a few moments the door of the great hall opened, and Geoffrey appeared at it, but without his lamp.

---

[4] lynch-pin (or linch-pin): *a pin lying transversely in an axle and holding a wheel in position*

[5] Visp: *a small town in the canton of Valais in Switzerland*

[6] What dost thou?: *(archaic) What are you doing?*

[7] thou art: *(archaic) you are*

'Hush!' he said, in a sort of whisper, and his voice was harsh and stern.

'Hush! Get to bed! I am working, and must not be disturbed. Go to sleep, and do not wake the house!'

With a chill in her heart – for the harshness of her husband's voice was new to her – she crept back to bed and lay there trembling, too frightened to cry, and listened to every sound.

There was a long pause of silence, and then the sound of some iron implement striking muffled blows! Then there came a clang of a heavy stone falling, followed by a muffled curse. Then a dragging sound, and then more noise of stone on stone.

She lay all the while in an agony of fear, and her heart beat dreadfully.

She heard a curious sort of scraping sound; and then there was silence.

Presently the door opened gently, and Geoffrey appeared.

His wife pretended to be asleep; but through her eyelashes she saw him wash from his hands something white that looked like lime.

In the morning he made no allusion to the previous night, and she was afraid to ask any question.

From that day there seemed some shadow over Geoffrey Brent. He neither ate nor slept as he had been accustomed, and his former habit of turning suddenly as though someone were speaking from behind him revived.

The old hall seemed to have some kind of fascination for him. He used to go there many times in the day, but grew impatient if anyone, even his wife, entered it. When the builder's foreman came to inquire about continuing his work Geoffrey was out driving; the man went into the hall, and when Geoffrey returned the servant told him of his arrival and where he was. With a frightful oath he pushed the servant aside and hurried up to the old hall.

The workman met him almost at the door; and as Geoffrey burst into the room he ran against him.

The man apologised: 'Beg pardon, sir, but I was just going out to make some enquiries. I directed twelve sacks of lime to be sent here, but I see there are only ten.'

'Damn the ten sacks and the twelve too!' was the ungracious and incomprehensible rejoinder.

The workman looked surprised, and tried to turn the conversation.

'I see, sir, there is a little matter which our people must have done; but the governor will of course see it set right at his own cost.'

'What do you mean?'

'That 'ere 'arth-stone[8], sir: Some idiot must have put a scaffold pole on it and cracked it right down the middle, and it's thick enough you'd think to stand hanythink[9].'

Geoffrey was silent for quite a minute, and then said in a constrained voice and with much gentler manner: 'Tell your people that I am not going on with the work in the hall at present. I want to leave it as it is for a while longer.'

'All right sir. I'll send up a few of our chaps to take away these poles and lime bags and tidy the place up a bit.'

'No! No!' said Geoffrey, 'leave them where they are. I shall send and tell you when you are to get on with the work.'

So the foreman went away, and his comment to his master was: 'I'd send in the bill, sir, for the work already done. Pears[10] to me that money's a little shaky in that quarter.'

Once or twice Delandre tried to stop Brent on the road, and, at last, finding that he could not attain his object rode after the carriage, calling out: 'What has become of my sister, your wife?' Geoffrey lashed his horses into a gallop, and the other, seeing from his white face and from his wife's collapse almost into a faint that his object was attained, rode away with a scowl and a laugh.

That night when Geoffrey went into the hall he passed over to the great fireplace, and all at once started back with a smothered cry.

Then with an effort he pulled himself together and went away, returning with a light. He bent down over the broken hearthstone to see if the moonlight falling through the storied window had in any way deceived him.

Then with a groan of anguish he sank to his knees. There, sure enough, through the crack in the broken stone were

---

[8] That 'ere 'arth-stone: *the workman means: 'this hearthstone here'*
[9] hanythink: *anything*
[10] Pears: *It appears*

protruding a multitude of threads of golden hair just tinged with grey! He was disturbed by a noise at the door, and looking round, saw his wife standing in the doorway.

In the desperation of the moment he took action to prevent discovery, and lighting a match at the lamp, stooped down and burned away the hair that rose through the broken stone.

Then rising nonchalantly as he could, he pretended surprise at seeing his wife beside him.

For the next week he lived in an agony; for, whether by accident or design, he could not find himself alone in the hall for any length of time.

At each visit the hair had grown afresh through the crack, and he had to watch it carefully lest his terrible secret should be discovered.

He tried to find a receptacle for the body of the murdered woman outside the house, but someone always interrupted him; and once, when he was coming out of the private doorway, he was met by his wife, who began to question him about it, and manifested surprise that she should not have before noticed the key which he now reluctantly showed her.

Geoffrey dearly and passionately loved his wife, so that any possibility of her discovering his dread secrets, or even of doubting him, filled him with anguish; and after a couple of days had passed, he could not help coming to the conclusion that, at least, she suspected something.

That very evening she came into the hall after her drive and found him there sitting moodily by the deserted fireplace.

She spoke to him directly.

'Geoffrey, I have been spoken to by that fellow Delandre, and he says horrible things. He tells to me that a week ago his sister returned to his house, the wreck and ruin of her former self, with only her golden hair as of old, and announced some fell intention.

He asked me where she is – and oh, Geoffrey, she is dead, she is dead! So how can she have returned? Oh! I am in dread, and I know not where to turn!'

For answer, Geoffrey burst into a torrent of blasphemy which made her shudder.

He cursed Delandre and his sister and all their kind, and in especial[11] he hurled curse after curse on her golden hair.

'Oh, hush! hush!' she said, and was then silent, for she feared her husband when she saw the evil effect of his humour.

Geoffrey in the torrent of his anger stood up and moved away from the hearth; but suddenly stopped as he saw a new look of terror in his wife's eyes.

He followed their glance, and then he too, shuddered – for there on the broken hearthstone lay a golden streak as the point of the hair rose though the crack.

'Look, look!' she shrieked. 'Is it some ghost of the dead? Come away – come away!' and seizing her husband by the wrist with the frenzy of madness, she pulled him from the room.

That night she was in a raging fever.

The doctor of the district attended to her at once, and special aid was telegraphed for to London.

Geoffrey was in despair, and in his anguish at the danger of his young wife almost forgot his own crime and its consequences.

In the evening the doctor had to leave to attend to others; but he left Geoffrey in charge of his wife.

His last words were: 'Remember, you must humour her till I come in the morning, or till some other doctor has her case in hand. What you have to dread is another attack of emotion. See that she is kept warm. Nothing more can be done.'

Late in the evening, when the rest of the household had retired, Geoffrey's wife got up from her bed and called to her husband.

'Come!' she said. 'Come to the old hall! I know where the gold comes from! I want to see it grow!'

Geoffrey would fain[12] have stopped her, but he feared for her life or reason on the one hand, and lest in a paroxysm she should shriek out her terrible suspicion, and seeing that it was useless to try to prevent her, wrapped a warm rug around her and went with her to the old hall.

---

[11] in especial: *in particular*
[12] fain *(archaic): willingly, gladly*

When they entered, she turned and shut the door and locked it.

'We want no strangers amongst us three tonight!' she whispered with a wan smile.

'We three! Nay[13] we are but two,' said Geoffrey with a shudder; he feared to say more.

'Sit here,' said his wife as she put out the light. 'Sit here by the hearth and watch the gold growing. The silver moonlight is jealous! See, it steals along the floor towards the gold – our gold!' Geoffrey looked with growing horror, and saw that during the hours that had passed the golden hair had protruded further through the broken hearthstone. He tried to hide it by placing his feet over the broken place; and his wife, drawing her chair beside him, leant over and laid her head on his shoulder.

'Now do not stir, dear,' she said; 'let us sit still and watch. We shall find the secret of the growing gold!' He passed his arm round her and sat silent; and as the moonlight stole along the floor she sank to sleep.

He feared to wake her; and so sat silent and miserable as the hours stole away. Before his horror-struck eyes the golden hair from the broken stone grew and grew; and as it increased, so his heart got colder and colder, till at last he had not power to stir, and sat with eyes full of terror watching his doom.

* * * * *

In the morning when the London doctor came, neither Geoffrey nor his wife could be found. Search was made in all the rooms, but without avail. As a last resource the great door of the old hall was broken open, and those who entered saw a grim and sorry sight. There by the deserted hearth Geoffrey Brent and his young wife sat cold and white and dead. Her face was peaceful, and her eyes were closed in sleep; but his face was a sight that made all who saw it shudder, for there was on it a look of unutterable horror.

The eyes were open and stared glassily at his feet, which were twined with tresses of golden hair, streaked with grey, which came through the broken hearthstone.

---

[13] nay *(archaic): no*

THE COMING OF ABEL BEHENNA

The little Cornish port of Pencastle was bright in the early April, when the sun had seemingly come to stay after a long and bitter winter.

Boldly and blackly the rock stood out against a background of shaded blue, where the sky fading into mist met the far horizon.

The sea was of true Cornish hue – sapphire, save where it became deep emerald green in the fathomless depths under the cliffs, where the seal caves opened their grim jaws.

On the slopes the grass was parched and brown. The spikes of furze bushes were ashy grey, but the golden yellow of their flowers streamed along the hillside, dipping out in lines as the rock cropped up, and lessening into patches and dots till finally it died away all together where the sea winds swept round the jutting cliffs and cut short the vegetation as though with an ever-working aerial shears.

The whole hillside, with its body of brown and flashes of yellow, was just like a colossal yellowhammer. The little harbour opened from the sea between towering cliffs, and behind a lonely rock, pierced with many caves and blowholes through which the sea in storm time sent its thunderous voice, together with a fountain of drifting spume.

Hence, it wound westwards in a serpentine course, guarded at its entrance by two little curving piers to left and right. These were roughly built of dark slates placed endways and held together with great beams bound with iron bands.

Thence, it flowed up the rocky bed of the stream whose winter torrents had of old cut out its way amongst the hills. This stream was deep at first, with here and there, where it widened, patches of broken rock exposed at low water, full of holes where crabs and lobsters were to be found at the ebb of the tide.

From amongst the rocks rose sturdy posts, used for warping in the little coasting vessels which frequented the port.

Higher up, the stream still flowed deeply, for the tide ran far inland, but always calmly for all the force of the wildest storm was broken below. Some quarter mile inland the stream was deep at high water, but at low tide there were at each side patches of the same broken rock as lower down, through the chinks of which the sweet water of the natural stream trickled and murmured after the tide had ebbed away.

Here, too, rose mooring posts for the fishermen's boats.

At either side of the river was a row of cottages down almost on the level of high tide. They were pretty cottages, strongly and snugly built, with trim narrow gardens in front, full of old-fashioned plants, flowering currants, coloured primroses, wallflower, and stonecrop.

Over the fronts of many of them climbed clematis and wisteria. The window sides and door posts of all were as white as snow, and the little pathway to each was paved with light coloured stones. At some of the doors were tiny porches, whilst at others were rustic seats cut from tree trunks or from old barrels; in nearly every case the window ledges were filled with boxes or pots of flowers or foliage plants.

Two men lived in cottages exactly opposite each other across the stream. Two men, both young, both good-looking, both prosperous, and who had been companions and rivals from their boyhood.

Abel Behenna was dark with the gypsy darkness which the Phoenician mining wanderers left in their track; Eric Sanson – which the local antiquarian said was a corruption of Sagamanson – was fair, with the ruddy hue which marked the path of the wild Norseman.

These two seemed to have singled out each other from the very beginning to work and strive together, to fight for each other and to stand back-to-back in all endeavours.

They had now put the coping-stone on their Temple of Unity by falling in love with the same girl.

Sarah Trefusis was certainly the prettiest girl in Pencastle, and there was many a young man who would gladly have tried his fortune with her, but that there were two to contend against, and each of these the strongest and most resolute man in the port – except the other.

The average young man thought that this was very hard, and on account of it bore no good will to either of the three principals: whilst the average young woman who had, lest worse should befall, to put up with the grumbling of her sweetheart, and the sense of being only second best which it implied, did not either, be sure, regard Sarah with friendly eye.

Thus it came, in the course of a year or so, for rustic courtship is a slow process, that the two men and woman found themselves thrown much together.

They were all satisfied, so it did not matter, and Sarah, who was vain and something frivolous, took care to have her revenge on both men and women in a quiet way.

When a young woman in her 'walking out' can only boast one not-quite-satisfied young man, it is no particular pleasure to her to see her escort cast sheep's eyes at a better-looking girl supported by two devoted swains.

At length there came a time which Sarah dreaded, and which she had tried to keep distant – the time when she had to make her choice between the two men.

She liked them both, and, indeed, either of them might have satisfied the ideas of even a more exacting girl. But her mind was so constituted that she thought more of what she might lose than of what she might gain; and whenever she thought she had made up her mind she became instantly assailed with doubts as to the wisdom of her choice. Always the man whom she had presumably lost became endowed afresh with a newer and more bountiful crop of advantages than had ever arisen from the possibility of his acceptance.

She promised each man that on her birthday she would give him his answer, and that day, the 11th of April, had now arrived. The promises had been given singly and confidentially, but each was given to a man who was not likely to forget.

Early in the morning she found both men hovering round her door. Neither had taken the other into his confidence, and each was simply seeking an early opportunity of getting his answer, and advancing his suit if necessary.

Damon, as a rule, does not take Pythias[1] with him when

---

[1] Damon… Pythias: *an allusion to the classical legend of two friends. Such was the depth of their loyalty that Damon offered himself as a hostage to save Pythias from execution.*

making a proposal; and in the heart of each man his own affairs had a claim far above any requirements of friendship. So, throughout the day, they kept seeing each other out.

The position was doubtless somewhat embarrassing to Sarah, and though the satisfaction of her vanity that she should be thus adored was very pleasing, yet there were moments when she was annoyed with both men for being so persistent.

Her only consolation at such moments was that she saw, through the elaborate smiles of the other girls when in passing they noticed her door thus doubly guarded, the jealousy which filled their hearts.

Sarah's mother was a person of commonplace and sordid ideas, and, seeing all along the state of affairs, her one intention, persistently expressed to her daughter in the plainest words, was to so arrange matters that Sarah should get all that was possible out of both men. With this purpose she had cunningly kept herself as far as possible in the background in the matter of her daughter's wooings, and watched in silence.

At first Sarah had been indignant with her for her sordid views; but, as usual, her weak nature gave way before persistence, and she had now got to the stage of acceptance.

She was not surprised when her mother whispered to her in the little yard behind the house: 'Go up the hillside for a while; I want to talk to these two. They're both red-hot for ye, and now's the time to get things fixed!' Sarah began a feeble remonstrance, but her mother cut her short:

'I tell ye, girl, that my mind is made up! Both these men want ye, and only one can have ye, but before ye choose it'll be so arranged that ye'll have all that both have got! Don't argy[2], child! Go up the hillside, and when ye come back I'll have it fixed – I see a way quite easy!'

So Sarah went up the hillside through the narrow paths between the golden furze, and Mrs Trefusis joined the two men in the living room of the little house. She opened the attack with the desperate courage which is in all mothers when they think for their children, howsoever mean the thoughts may be: 'Ye two men, ye're both in love with my

---

[2] argy: *argue*

Sarah!' Their bashful silence gave consent to the barefaced proposition.

She went on: 'Neither of ye has much!' Again they tacitly acquiesced in the soft impeachment. 'I don't know that either of ye could keep a wife!' Though neither said a word their looks and bearing expressed distinct dissent.

Mrs Trefusis went on: 'But if ye'd put what ye both have together ye'd make a comfortable home for one of ye – and Sarah!' She eyed the men keenly, with her cunning eyes half shut as she spoke; then satisfied from her scrutiny that the idea was accepted she went on quickly, as if to prevent argument:

'The girl likes ye both, and mayhap[3] it's hard for her to choose. Why don't ye toss up for her? First put your money together – ye've each got a bit put by, I know. Let the lucky man take the lot and trade with it a bit, and then come home and marry her. Neither of ye's afraid, I suppose! And neither of ye'll say that he won't do that much for the girl that ye both say ye love!'

Abel broke the silence: 'It don't seem the square thing to toss for the girl! She wouldn't like it herself, and it doesn't seem – seem respectful like to her.'

Eric interrupted. He was conscious that his chance was not so good as Abel's in case Sarah should wish to choose between them: 'Are ye afraid of the hazard?'

'Not me!' said Abel, boldly.

Mrs Trefusis, seeing that her idea was beginning to work, followed up the advantage: 'It is settled that ye put yer money together to make a home for her, whether ye toss for her or leave it for her to choose?'

'Yes,' said Eric quickly, and Abel agreed with equal sturdiness.

Mrs Trefusis' little, cunning eyes twinkled. She heard Sarah's step in the yard, and said: 'Well! here she comes, and I leave it to her.' And she went out.

During her brief walk on the hillside Sarah had been trying to make up her mind. She was feeling almost angry with both men for being the cause of her difficulty, and as she came into the room said shortly: 'I want to have a word

---

[3] mayhap: *(archaic)* perhaps

with you both – come to the Flagstaff Rock, where we can be alone.'

She took her hat and went out of the house up the winding path to the steep rock crowned with a high flagstaff, where once the wreckers' fire basket used to burn. This was the rock which formed the northern jaw of the little harbour.

There was only room on the path for two abreast, and it marked the state of things pretty well when, by a sort of implied arrangement, Sarah went first, and the two men followed, walking abreast and keeping step. By this time, each man's heart was boiling with jealousy.

When they came to the top of the rock, Sarah stood against the flagstaff, and the two young men stood opposite her. She had chosen her position with knowledge and intention, for there was no room for anyone to stand beside her.

They were all silent for a while; then Sarah began to laugh and said: 'I promised the both of you to give you an answer today. I've been thinking and thinking and thinking, till I began to get angry with you both for plaguing me so; and even now I don't seem any nearer than ever I was to making up my mind.'

Eric said suddenly: 'Let us toss for it, lass!'

Sarah showed no indignation whatever at the proposition; her mother's eternal suggestion had schooled her to the acceptance of something of the kind, and her weak nature made it easy to her to grasp at any way out of the difficulty.

She stood with downcast eyes idly picking at the sleeve of her dress, seeming to have tacitly acquiesced in the proposal.

Both men instinctively realising this pulled each a coin from his pocket, spun it in the air, and dropped his other hand over the palm on which it lay.

For a few seconds they remained thus, all silent; then Abel, who was the more thoughtful of the men, spoke: 'Sarah! Is this good?' As he spoke he removed the upper hand from the coin and placed the latter back in his pocket.

Sarah was nettled: 'Good or bad, it's good enough for me! Take it or leave it as you like,' she said, to which he replied quickly:

'Nay lass! Aught that concerns you is good enow[4] for me. I did but think of you lest you might have pain or disappointment hereafter. If you love Eric better than me, in God's name say so, and I think I'm man enow to stand aside. Likewise, if I'm the one, don't make us both miserable for life!'

Face to face with a difficulty, Sarah's weak nature proclaimed itself; she put her hands before her face and began to cry, saying: 'It was my mother. She keeps telling me!'

The silence which followed was broken by Eric, who said hotly to Abel: 'Let the lass alone, can't you? If she wants to choose this way, let her. It's good enough for me – and for you, too! She's said it now, and must abide by it!'

Hereupon Sarah turned upon him in sudden fury, and cried: 'Hold your tongue! what is it to you, at any rate?' and she resumed her crying.

Eric was so flabbergasted that he had not a word to say, but stood looking particularly foolish, with his mouth open and his hands held out with the coin still between them.

All were silent till Sarah, taking her hands from her face laughed hysterically and said: 'As you two can't make up your minds, I'm going home!' and she turned to go.

'Stop,' said Abel, in an authoritative voice.

'Eric, you hold the coin, and I'll cry. Now, before we settle it, let us clearly understand: the man who wins takes all the money that we both have got, brings it to Bristol and ships on a voyage and trades with it.

Then he comes back and marries Sarah, and they two keep all, whatever there may be, as the result of the trading.

Is this what we understand?'

'Yes,' said Eric.

'I'll marry him on my next birthday,' said Sarah.

Having said it the intolerably mercenary spirit of her action seemed to strike her, and impulsively she turned away with a bright blush.

Fire seemed to sparkle in the eyes of both men.

---

[4] enow: *(archaic) enough*

Said Eric: 'A year so be! The man that wins is to have one year.'

'Toss!' cried Abel, and the coin spun in the air.

Eric caught it, and again held it between his outstretched hands.

'Heads!' cried Abel, a pallor sweeping over his face as he spoke.

As he leaned forwards to look Sarah leaned forwards too, and their heads almost touched.

He could feel her hair blowing on his cheek, and it thrilled through him like fire.

Eric lifted his upper hand; the coin lay with its head up.

Abel stepped forward and took Sarah in his arms.

With a curse Eric hurled the coin far into the sea. Then he leaned against the flagstaff and scowled at the others with his hands thrust deep into his pockets.

Abel whispered wild words of passion and delight into Sarah's ears, and as she listened she began to believe that fortune had rightly interpreted the wishes of her secret heart, and that she loved Abel best. Presently Abel looked up and caught sight of Eric's face as the last ray of sunset struck it. The red light intensified the natural ruddiness of his complexion, and he looked as though he were steeped in blood.

Abel did not mind his scowl, for now that his own heart was at rest he could feel unalloyed pity for his friend.

He stepped over meaning to comfort him, and held out his hand, saying:

'It was my chance, old lad. Don't grudge it me. I'll try to make Sarah a happy woman, and you shall be a brother to us both!'

'Brother be damned!' was all the answer Eric made, as he turned away.

When he had gone a few steps down the rocky path he turned and came back. Standing before Abel and Sarah, who had their arms round each other, he said:

'You have a year. Make the most of it! And be sure you're in time to claim your wife! Be back to have your banns up in time to be married on the 11th of April. If you're not, I tell you I shall have my banns up, and you may get back too late.'

'What do you mean, Eric? You are mad!'

'No more mad than you are, Abel Behenna. You go, that's

your chance! I stay, that's mine! I don't mean to let the grass grow under my feet. Sarah cared no more for you than for me five minutes ago, and she may come back to that five minutes after you're gone! You won by a point only – the game may change.'

'The game won't change!' said Abel shortly. 'Sarah, you'll be true to me? You won't marry till I return?'

'For a year!' added Eric, quickly, 'that's the bargain.'

'I promise for the year,' said Sarah.

A dark look came over Abel's face, and he was about to speak, but he mastered himself and smiled:

'I mustn't be too hard or get angry tonight! Come, Eric! we played and fought together. I won fairly. I played fairly all the game of our wooing! You know that as well as I do; and now when I am going away, I shall look to my old and true comrade to help me when I am gone!'

'I'll help you none,' said Eric, 'so help me God!'

'It was God helped me,' said Abel simply.

'Then let Him go on helping you,' said Eric angrily. 'The Devil is good enough for me!' and without another word he rushed down the steep path and disappeared behind the rocks.

When he had gone Abel hoped for some tender passage with Sarah, but the first remark she made chilled him. 'How lonely it all seems without Eric!' and this note sounded till he had left her at home – and after.

Early on the next morning Abel heard a noise at his door, and on going out saw Eric walking rapidly away: a small canvas bag full of gold and silver lay on the threshold; on a small slip of paper pinned to it was written:

'Take the money and go. I stay. God for you!
The Devil for me! Remember the 11th of April.
　　　　　　　　　　　　　　　　–ERIC SANSON.'

That afternoon Abel went off to Bristol, and a week later sailed on the *Star of the Sea* bound for Pahang[5].

His money – including that which had been Eric's – was on board in the shape of a venture of cheap toys.

He had been advised by a shrewd old mariner of Bristol whom he knew, and who knew the ways of the

---

[5] Pahang: *a West Malaysian state, lying on the South China Sea*

Chersonese[6], who predicted that every penny invested would be returned with a shilling to boot.

As the year wore on Sarah became more and more disturbed in her mind. Eric was always at hand to make love to her in his own persistent, masterful manner, and to this she did not object.

Only one letter came from Abel, to say that his venture had proved successful, and that he had sent some two hundred pounds to the bank at Bristol, and was trading with fifty pounds still remaining in goods for China, whither[7] the *Star of the Sea* was bound and whence[8] she would return to Bristol. He suggested that Eric's share of the venture should be returned to him with his share of the profits. This proposition was treated with anger by Eric, and as simply childish by Sarah's mother.

More than six months had since then elapsed, but no other letter had come, and Eric's hopes which had been dashed down by the letter from Pahang, began to rise again.

He perpetually assailed Sarah with an 'if!' If Abel did not return, would she then marry him? If the 11th of April went by without Abel being in the port, would she give him over? If Abel had taken his fortune, and married another girl on the head of it, would she marry him, Eric, as soon as the truth were known? And so on in an endless variety of possibilities.

The power of the strong will and the determined purpose over the woman's weaker nature became in time manifest. Sarah began to lose her faith in Abel and to regard Eric as a possible husband; and a possible husband is, in a woman's eye, different to all other men. A new affection for him began to arise in her breast, and the daily familiarities of permitted courtship furthered the growing affection.

Sarah began to regard Abel as rather a rock in the road of her life, and had it not been for her mother's constantly reminding her of the good fortune already laid by in the Bristol Bank she would have tried to have shut her eyes altogether to the fact of Abel's existence. The 11th of April

---

[6] Chersonese: *(poetic) peninsula,* here, *the Malay peninsula*

[7] whither : *(archaic) where, to what place*

[8] whence : *(archaic) from where, from what place*

was Saturday, so that in order to have the marriage on that day it would be necessary that the banns should be called on Sunday, the 22nd of March.

From the beginning of that month Eric kept perpetually on the subject of Abel's absence, and his outspoken opinion that the latter was either dead or married began to become a reality to the woman's mind.

As the first half of the month wore on Eric became more jubilant, and after church on the fifteenth he took Sarah for a walk to the Flagstaff Rock. There he asserted himself strongly:

'I told Abel, and you too, that if he was not here to put up his banns in time for the eleventh, I would put up mine for the twelfth. Now the time has come when I mean to do it. He hasn't kept his word.'

Here Sarah struck in out of her weakness and indecision: 'He hasn't broken it yet!'

Eric ground his teeth with anger: 'If you mean to stick up for him,' he said, as he smote his hands savagely on the flagstaff, which sent forth a shivering murmur, 'well and good. I'll keep my part of the bargain. On Sunday I shall give notice of the banns, and you can deny them in the church if you will. If Abel is in Pencastle on the eleventh, he can have them cancelled, and his own put up; but till then, I take my course, and woe to anyone who stands in my way!'

With that he flung himself down the rocky pathway, and Sarah could not but admire his Viking strength and spirit, as, crossing the hill, he strode away along the cliffs towards Bude.

During the week no news was heard of Abel, and on Saturday Eric gave notice of the banns of marriage between himself and Sarah Trefusis.

The clergyman would have remonstrated with him, for although nothing formal had been told to the neighbours, it had been understood since Abel's departure that on his return he was to marry Sarah; but Eric would not discuss the question: 'It is a painful subject, sir,' he said with a firmness which the parson, who was a very young man, could not but be swayed by. 'Surely there is nothing against Sarah or me. Why should there be any bones made about the matter?' The parson said no more, and on the next day he read out the banns for the first time amidst an audible buzz from the congregation.

Sarah was present, contrary to custom, and though she blushed furiously enjoyed her triumph over the other girls whose banns had not yet come.

Before the week was over she began to make her wedding dress. Eric used to come and look at her at work and the sight thrilled through him. He used to say all sorts of pretty things to her at such times, and there were to both delicious moments of love-making. The banns were read a second time on the twenty-ninth, and Eric's hope grew more and more fixed though there were to him moments of acute despair when he realised that the cup of happiness might be dashed from his lips at any moment, right up to the last.

At such times he was full of passion – desperate and remorseless – and he ground his teeth and clenched his hands in a wild way as though some taint of the old Berserker[9] fury of his ancestors still lingered in his blood.

On the Thursday of that week he looked in on Sarah and found her, amid a flood of sunshine, putting finishing touches to her white wedding gown.

His own heart was full of gaiety, and the sight of the woman who was so soon to be his own so occupied, filled him with a joy unspeakable, and he felt faint with languorous ecstasy.

Bending over he kissed Sarah on the mouth, and then whispered in her rosy ear: 'Your wedding dress, Sarah! And for me!'

As he drew back to admire her she looked up saucily, and said to him: 'Perhaps not for you. There is more than a week yet for Abel!' and then cried out in dismay, for with a wild gesture and a fierce oath Eric dashed out of the house, banging the door behind him.

The incident disturbed Sarah more than she could have thought possible, for it awoke all her fears and doubts and indecision afresh. She cried a little, and put by her dress,

---

[9] Berserker: *the Berserkers were ancient Norse warriors who worked themselves into a frenzy before going into battle, when they would fight with extreme fury. This word gives rise to the English expression 'to go beserk' meaning to become enraged.*

and to soothe herself went out to sit for a while on the summit of the Flagstaff Rock.

When she arrived she found there a little group anxiously discussing the weather. The sea was calm and the sun bright, but across the sea were strange lines of darkness and light, and close in to shore the rocks were fringed with foam, which spread out in great white curves and circles as the currents drifted. The wind had backed, and came in sharp, cold puffs. The blow-hole, which ran under the Flagstaff Rock, from the rocky bay without to the harbour within, was booming at intervals, and the seagulls were screaming ceaselessly as they wheeled about the entrance of the port.

'It looks bad,' she heard an old fisherman say to the coastguard. 'I seen it just like this once before, when the East Indiaman[10] *Coromandel* went to pieces in Dizzard Bay!'

Sarah did not wait to hear more. She was of a timid nature where danger was concerned, and could not bear to hear of wrecks and disasters. She went home and resumed the completion of her dress, secretly determined to appease Eric when she should meet him with a sweet apology – and to take the earliest opportunity of being even with him after her marriage.

The old fisherman's weather prophecy was justified. That night at dusk a wild storm came on. The sea rose and lashed the western coasts from Skye to Scilly and left a tale of disaster everywhere.

The sailors and fishermen of Pencastle all turned out on the rocks and cliffs and watched eagerly. Presently, by a flash of lightning, a ketch was seen drifting under only a jib about half a mile outside the port.

All eyes and all glasses were concentrated on her, waiting for the next flash, and when it came a chorus went up that it was the *Lovely Alice*, trading between Bristol and Penzance, and touching at all the little ports between.

'God help them!' said the harbour-master, 'for nothing in this world can save them when they are between Bude and Tintagel and the wind on shore!'

---

[10] East Indiaman: *a ship operating under charter or licence to any of the European East India Companies that traded with Southeast Asia, East Asia, and India between the 17th and 19th centuries*

The coastguards exerted themselves, and, aided by brave hearts and willing hands, they brought the rocket apparatus up on the summit of the Flagstaff Rock. Then they burned blue lights so that those on board might see the harbour opening in case they could make any effort to reach it.

They worked gallantly enough on board; but no skill or strength of man could avail. Before many minutes were over the *Lovely Alice* rushed to her doom on the great island rock that guarded the mouth of the port. The screams of those on board were faintly borne on the tempest as they flung themselves into the sea in a last chance for life.

The blue lights were kept burning, and eager eyes peered into the depths of the waters in case any face could be seen; and ropes were held ready to fling out in aid. But never a face was seen, and the willing arms rested idle.

Eric was there amongst his fellows. His old Icelandic origin was never more apparent than in that wild hour. He took a rope, and shouted in the ear of the harbour-master: 'I shall go down on the rock over the seal cave. The tide is running up, and someone may drift in there!'

'Keep back, man!' came the answer. 'Are you mad? One slip on that rock and you are lost: and no man could keep his feet in the dark on such a place in such a tempest!'

'Not a bit,' came the reply. 'You remember how Abel Behenna saved me there on a night like this when my boat went on the Gull Rock. He dragged me up from the deep water in the seal cave, and now someone may drift in there again as I did,' and he was gone into the darkness.

The projecting rock hid the light on the Flagstaff Rock, but he knew his way too well to miss it. His boldness and sureness of foot standing to him, he shortly stood on the great round-topped rock cut away beneath by the action of the waves over the entrance of the seal cave, where the water was fathomless.

There he stood in comparative safety, for the concave shape of the rock beat back the waves with their own force, and though the water below him seemed to boil like a seething cauldron, just beyond the spot there was a space of almost calm. The rock, too, seemed here to shut off the sound of the gale, and he listened as well as watched.

As he stood there ready, with his coil of rope poised to throw, he thought he heard below him, just beyond the whirl of the water, a faint, despairing cry. He echoed it with a shout that rang into the night. Then he waited for the flash of lightning, and as it passed flung his rope out into the darkness where he had seen a face rising through the swirl of the foam. The rope was caught, for he felt a pull on it, and he shouted again in his mighty voice: 'Tie it round your waist, and I shall pull you up.' Then, when he felt that it was fast, he moved along the rock to the far side of the sea cave, where the deep water was something stiller, and where he could get foothold secure enough to drag the rescued man on the overhanging rock.

He began to pull, and shortly he knew from the rope taken in that the man he was now rescuing must soon be close to the top of the rock. He steadied himself for a moment, and drew a long breath, that he might at the next effort complete the rescue. He had just bent his back to the work when a flash of lightning revealed to each other the two men – the rescuer and the rescued. Eric Sanson and Abel Behenna were face to face – and none knew of the meeting save themselves; and God.

On the instant a wave of passion swept through Eric's heart. All his hopes were shattered, and with the hatred of Cain[11] his eyes looked out. He saw in the instant of recognition the joy in Abel's face that his was the hand to succour him, and this intensified his hate. Whilst the passion was on him he started back, and the rope ran out between his hands. His moment of hate was followed by an impulse of his better manhood, but it was too late. Before he could recover himself, Abel encumbered with the rope that should have aided him, was plunged with a despairing cry back into the darkness of the devouring sea. Then, feeling all the madness and the doom of Cain upon him, Eric rushed back over the rocks, heedless of the danger and eager only for one thing – to be amongst other people whose living noises would shut out that last cry which seemed to ring still in his ears.

When he regained the Flagstaff Rock the men surrounded him, and through the fury of the storm he heard the harbour

---

[11] Cain: *(Old Testament) son of Adam and Eve, who murdered his brother Abel out of jealousy*

master say: 'We feared you were lost when we heard a cry! How white you are! Where is your rope? Was there anyone drifted in?'

'No one,' he shouted in answer, for he felt that he could never explain that he had let his old comrade slip back into the sea, and at the very place and under the very circumstances in which that comrade had saved his own life. He hoped by one bold lie to set the matter at rest for ever. There was no one to bear witness – and if he should have to carry that still white face in his eyes and that despairing cry in his ears for evermore – at least none should know of it.

'No one,' he cried, more loudly still. 'I slipped on the rock, and the rope fell into the sea!' So saying he left them, and, rushing down the steep path, gained his own cottage and locked himself within.

The remainder of that night he passed lying on his bed – dressed and motionless – staring upwards, and seeming to see through the darkness a pale face gleaming wet in the lightning, with its glad recognition turning to ghastly despair, and to hear a cry which never ceased to echo in his soul. In the morning the storm was over and all was smiling again, except that the sea was still boisterous with its unspent fury.

Great pieces of wreck drifted into the port, and the sea around the island rock was strewn with others. Two bodies also drifted into the harbour – one the master of the wrecked ketch, the other a strange seaman whom no one knew.

Sarah saw nothing of Eric till the evening, and then he only looked in for a minute. He did not come into the house, but simply put his head in through the open window: 'Well, Sarah,' he called out in a loud voice, though to her it did not ring truly, 'is the wedding dress done? Sunday week, mind! Sunday week!'

Sarah was glad to have the reconciliation so easy; but, womanlike, when she saw the storm was over and her own fears groundless, she at once repeated the cause of offence. 'Sunday so be it,' she said without looking up, 'if Abel isn't there on Saturday!' Then she looked up saucily, though her heart was full of fear of another outburst on the part of her impetuous lover. But the window was empty; Eric had taken himself off, and with a pout she resumed her work.

She saw Eric no more till Sunday afternoon, after the banns had been called the third time, when he came up to her before all the people with an air of proprietorship which half pleased and half annoyed her.

'Not yet, mister!' she said, pushing him away, as the other girls giggled. 'Wait till Sunday next, if you please – the day after Saturday!' she added, looking at him saucily.

The girls giggled again, and the young men guffawed. They thought it was the snub that touched him so that he became as white as a sheet as he turned away. But Sarah, who knew more than they did, laughed, for she saw triumph through the spasm of pain that overspread his face.

The week passed uneventfully; however, as Saturday drew nigh Sarah had occasional moments of anxiety, and as to Eric he went about at night-time like a man possessed. He restrained himself when others were by, but now and again he went down amongst the rocks and caves and shouted aloud. This seemed to relieve him somewhat, and he was better able to restrain himself for some time after.

All Saturday he stayed in his own house and never left it. As he was to be married on the morrow, the neighbours thought it was shyness on his part, and did not trouble or notice him. Only once was he disturbed, and that was when the chief boatman came to him and sat down, and after a pause said:

'Eric, I was over in Bristol yesterday. I was in the ropemaker's getting a coil to replace the one you lost the night of the storm, and there I saw Michael Heavens of this place, who is a salesman there. He told me that Abel Behenna had come home the week ere last on the *Star of the Sea* from Canton, and that he had lodged a sight of money in the Bristol Bank in the name of Sarah Behenna. He told Michael so himself – and that he had taken passage on the *Lovely Alice* to Pencastle.

'Bear up, man,' for Eric had with a groan dropped his head on his knees, with his face between his hands. 'He was your old comrade, I know, but you couldn't help him. He must have gone down with the rest that awful night. I thought I'd better tell you, lest it might come some other way, and you might keep Sarah Trefusis from being frightened. They were good friends once, and women take these things to heart. It would not do to let her be pained with such a thing on her wedding day!' Then he rose and went away, leaving Eric still sitting disconsolately with his head on his knees.

'Poor fellow!' murmured the chief boatman to himself; 'he takes it to heart. Well, well! right enough! They were true comrades once, and Abel saved him!'

The afternoon of that day, when the children had left school, they strayed as usual on half-holidays along the quay and the paths by the cliffs. Presently some of them came running in a state of great excitement to the harbour, where a few men were unloading a coal ketch, and a great many were superintending the operation. One of the children called out:

'There is a porpoise in the harbour mouth! We saw it come through the blow-hole! It had a long tail, and was deep under the water!'

'It was no porpoise,' said another; 'it was a seal; but it had a long tail! It came out of the seal cave!'

The other children bore various testimony, but on two points they were unanimous – it, whatever 'it' was, had come through the blow-hole deep under the water, and had a long, thin tail – a tail so long that they could not see the end of it.

There was much unmerciful chaffing of the children by the men on this point, but as it was evident that they had seen something, quite a number of persons, young and old, male and female, went along the high paths on either side of the harbour mouth to catch a glimpse of this new addition to the fauna of the sea, a long-tailed porpoise or seal.

The tide was now coming in. There was a slight breeze, and the surface of the water was rippled so that it was only at moments that anyone could see clearly into the deep water.

After a spell of watching a woman called out that she saw something moving up the channel, just below where she was standing.

There was a stampede to the spot, but by the time the crowd had gathered the breeze had freshened, and it was impossible to see with any distinctness below the surface of the water.

On being questioned the woman described what she had seen, but in such an incoherent way that the whole thing was put down as an effect of imagination; had it not been for the children's report she would not have been credited at all.

Her semi-hysterical statement that what she saw was 'like a pig with the entrails out' was only thought anything of by an old coastguard, who shook his head but did not make any remark.

For the remainder of the daylight this man was seen always on the bank, looking into the water, but always with disappointment manifest on his face.

Eric arose early on the next morning – he had not slept all night, and it was a relief to him to move about in the light.

He shaved himself with a hand that did not tremble, and dressed himself in his wedding clothes. There was a haggard look on his face, and he seemed as though he had grown years older in the last few days. Still there was a wild, uneasy light of triumph in his eyes, and he kept murmuring to himself over and over again: 'This is my wedding-day! Abel cannot claim her now – living or dead! – living or dead! – living or dead!'

He sat in his armchair, waiting with an uncanny quietness for the church hour to arrive.

When the bell began to ring he arose and passed out of his house, closing the door behind him.

He looked at the river and saw the tide had just turned.

In the church he sat with Sarah and her mother, holding Sarah's hand tightly in his all the time, as though he feared to lose her.

When the service was over they stood up together, and were married in the presence of the entire congregation; for no one left the church. Both made the responses clearly – Eric's being even on the defiant side.

When the wedding was over Sarah took her husband's arm, and they walked away together, the boys and younger girls being cuffed by their elders into a decorous behaviour, for they would fain have followed close behind their heels. The way from the church led down to the back of Eric's cottage, a narrow passage being between it and that of his next neighbour. When the bridal couple had passed through this the remainder of the congregation, who had followed them at a little distance, were startled by a long, shrill scream from the bride.

They rushed through the passage and found her on the bank with wild eyes, pointing to the river bed opposite Eric Sanson's door.

The falling tide had deposited there the body of Abel Behenna stark upon the broken rocks.

The rope trailing from its waist had been twisted by the current round the mooring post, and had held it back whilst the tide had ebbed away from it.

The right elbow had fallen in a chink in the rock, leaving the hand outstretched towards Sarah, with the open palm upwards as though it were extended to receive hers, the pale drooping fingers open to the clasp.

All that happened afterwards was never quite known to Sarah Sanson. Whenever she would try to recollect there would become a buzzing in her ears and a dimness in her eyes, and all would pass away. The only thing that she could remember of it all – and this she never forgot – was Eric's breathing heavily, with his face whiter than that of the dead man, as he muttered under his breath: 'Devil's help! Devil's faith! Devil's price!'

THE BURIAL OF THE RATS

Leaving Paris by the Orléans road, cross the Enceinte[1], and, turning to the right, you find yourself in a somewhat wild and not at all savoury district. Right and left, before and behind, on every side rise great heaps of dust and waste accumulated by the process of time.

Paris has its night as well as its day life, and the sojourner who enters his hotel in the Rue de Rivoli or the Rue Saint Honoré late at night or leaves it early in the morning, can guess, in coming near Montrouge – if he has not done so already – the purpose of those great waggons that look like boilers on wheels which he finds halting everywhere as he passes.

Every city has its peculiar institutions created out of its own needs; and one of the most notable institutions of Paris is its rag-picking population. In the early morning – and Parisian life commences at an early hour – may be seen in most streets standing on the pathway opposite every court and alley and between every few houses, as still in some American cities, even in parts of New York, large wooden boxes into which the domestics or tenement-holders empty the accumulated dust of the past day. Round these boxes gather and pass on, when the work is done, to fresh fields of labour and pastures new, squalid, hungry-looking men and women, the implements of whose craft consist of a coarse bag or basket slung over the shoulder and a little rake with which they turn over and probe and examine in the minutest manner the dustbins. They pick up and deposit in their baskets, by aid of their rakes, whatever they may find, with the same facility as a Chinaman uses his chopsticks.

Paris is a city of centralisation – and centralisation and classification are closely allied. In the early times, when centralisation is becoming a fact, its forerunner is classification. All things which are similar or analogous become grouped together, and from the grouping of groups rises one whole or central point. We see radiating many long arms with innumerable tentaculae, and in the centre rises a

---

[1] Enceinte: *a boundary wall* (here, *the wall enclosing and serving to defend the city of Paris*)

gigantic head with a comprehensive brain and keen eyes to look on every side and ears sensitive to hear – and a voracious mouth to swallow.

Other cities resemble all the birds and beasts and fishes whose appetites and digestions are normal. Paris alone is the analogical apotheosis of the octopus. Product of centralisation carried to an *ad absurdum*, it fairly represents the devil fish; and in no respects is the resemblance more curious than in the similarity of the digestive apparatus.

Those intelligent tourists who, having surrendered their individuality into the hands of Messrs Cook or Gaze[2], 'do' Paris in three days, are often puzzled to know how it is that the dinner which in London would cost about six shillings, can be had for three francs in a café in the Palais Royal. They need have no more wonder if they will but consider the classification which is a theoretic speciality of Parisian life, and adopt all round the fact from which the chiffonier[3] has his genesis.

The Paris of 1850 was not like the Paris of today, and those who see the Paris of Napoleon and Baron Haussmann[4] can hardly realise the existence of the state of things forty-five years ago.

Amongst other things, however, which have not changed are those districts where the waste is gathered. Dust is dust all the world over, in every age, and the family likeness of dustheaps is perfect. The traveller, therefore, who visits the environs of Montrouge can go back in fancy without difficulty to the year 1850.

In this year I was making a prolonged stay in Paris. I was very much in love with a young lady who, though she returned my passion, so far yielded to the wishes of her parents that she had promised not to see me or to correspond with me for a year. I, too, had been compelled to accede to these conditions under a vague hope of parental approval. During the term of probation I had promised to

---

[2] Messrs Cook or Gaze: *a reference to Thomas Cook, creator of one of the first travel companies, and his competitor, Henry Gaze.*
[3] chiffonier: *rag-picker*
[4] Baron Haussmann: *Baron Georges-Eugène Haussmann (1809-1891), French urban planner responsible for modernising Paris, giving it its now familiar hub-and-spoke geometry and long, straight avenues and boulevards.*

remain out of the country and not to write to my dear one until the expiration of the year.

Naturally the time went heavily with me. There was no one of my own family or circle who could tell me of Alice, and none of her own folk had, I am sorry to say, sufficient generosity to send me even an occasional word of comfort regarding her health and well-being. I spent six months wandering about Europe, but as I could find no satisfactory distraction in travel, I determined to come to Paris, where, at least, I would be within easy hail of London in case any good fortune should call me thither[5] before the appointed time. That 'hope deferred maketh the heart sick[6]' was never better exemplified than in my case, for in addition to the perpetual longing to see the face I loved there was always with me a harrowing anxiety lest some accident should prevent me showing Alice in due time that I had, throughout the long period of probation, been faithful to her trust and my own love. Thus, every adventure which I undertook had a fierce pleasure of its own, for it was fraught with possible consequences greater than it would have ordinarily borne.

Like all travellers I exhausted the places of most interest in the first month of my stay, and was driven in the second month to look for amusement whithersoever[7] I might. Having made sundry journeys to the better-known suburbs, I began to see that there was a *terra incognita*, in so far as the guide book was concerned, in the social wilderness lying between these attractive points. Accordingly I began to systematise my researches, and each day took up the thread of my exploration at the place where I had on the previous day dropped it.

In the process of time my wanderings led me near Montrouge, and I saw that hereabouts lay the Ultima Thule[8]

---

[5] thither: *(archaic): there*

[6] hope deferred maketh the heart sick: *Biblical quotation, in full: 'Hope deferred maketh the heart sick: but when the desire cometh, it is a tree of life.' (Proverbs 13.12)*

[7] whithersoever: *(archaic): wherever*

[8] Ultima Thule: *Thule is the name given by ancient geographers to an alleged island (possibly somewhere north of Britain) regarded by them as the most northerly limit of the habitable globe; figuratively, the expression means an ultimate objective.*

of social exploration – a country as little known as that round the source of the White Nile[9]. And so I determined to investigate philosophically the chiffonier – his habitat, his life, and his means of life.

The job was an unsavoury one, difficult of accomplishment, and with little hope of adequate reward. However, despite reason, obstinacy prevailed, and I entered into my new investigation with a keener energy than I could have summoned to aid me in any investigation leading to any end, valuable or worthy.

One day, late in a fine afternoon, towards the end of September, I entered the holy of holies of the city of dust. The place was evidently the recognised abode of a number of chiffoniers, for some sort of arrangement was manifested in the formation of the dustheaps near the road. I passed amongst these heaps, which stood like orderly sentries, determined to penetrate further and trace dust to its ultimate location.

As I passed along I saw behind the dustheaps a few forms that flitted to and fro, evidently watching with interest the advent of any stranger to such a place. The district was like a small Switzerland, and as I went forwards my tortuous course shut out the path behind me.

Presently I got into what seemed a small city or community of chiffoniers. There were a number of shanties or huts, such as may be met with in the remote parts of the Bog of Allen[10] – rude places with wattled walls, plastered with mud and roofs of rude thatch made from stable refuse – such places as one would not like to enter for any consideration, and which even in watercolour could only look picturesque if judiciously treated. In the midst of these huts was one of the strangest adaptations – I cannot say habitations – I had ever seen. An immense old wardrobe, the colossal remnant of some boudoir of Charles VII, or Henry II[11], had been converted into a dwelling-house. The double

---

[9] White Nile: *a tributary of the Nile. The nineteenth-century quest by Europeans to discover the source of the Nile was concentrated on the White Nile and became symbolic of their penetration and exploration of the heart of Africa.*

[10] Bog of Allen: *an extensive peat bog located in the centre of Ireland*

[11] Charles VII, or Henry II: *two kings of France in the fifteenth and sixteenth centuries, respectively*

doors lay open, so that the entire ménage was open to public view. In the open half of the wardrobe was a common sitting room of some four feet by six, in which sat, smoking their pipes round a charcoal brazier, no fewer than six old soldiers of the First Republic[12], with their uniforms torn and worn threadbare. Evidently they were of the *mauvais sujet*[13] class; their blear eyes and limp jaws told plainly of a common love of absinthe; and their eyes had that haggard, worn look which stamps the drunkard at his worst, and that look of slumbering ferocity which follows hard in the wake of drink. The other side stood as of old, with its shelves intact, save that they were cut to half their depth, and in each shelf, of which there were six, was a bed made with rags and straw. The half-dozen of worthies who inhabited this structure looked at me curiously as I passed; and when I looked back after going a little way I saw their heads together in a whispered conference. I did not like the look of this at all, for the place was very lonely, and the men looked very, very villainous. However, I did not see any cause for fear, and went on my way, penetrating further and further into the Sahara. The way was tortuous to a degree, and from going round in a series of semi-circles, as one goes in skating with the Dutch roll, I got rather confused with regard to the points of the compass.

When I had penetrated a little way I saw, as I turned the corner of a half-made heap, sitting on a heap of straw an old soldier with threadbare coat.

'Hallo!' said I to myself; 'the First Republic is well represented here in its soldiery.'

As I passed him the old man never even looked up at me, but gazed on the ground with stolid persistency. Again I remarked to myself: 'See what a life of rude warfare can do! This old man's curiosity is a thing of the past.'

When I had gone a few steps, however, I looked back suddenly, and saw that curiosity was not dead, for the veteran had raised his head and was regarding me with a

---

[12] the First Republic: *the republic founded in France following the abolition of the monarchy in 1792. The First Republic lasted until 1804, the year that brought the establishment of the First French Empire under Napoleon Bonaparte.*

[13] mauvais sujet: *(French) bad fellow. The narrator is saying that they were clearly disreputable characters.*

very queer expression. He seemed to me to look very like one of the six worthies in the press. When he saw me looking he dropped his head; and without thinking further of him I went on my way, satisfied that there was a strange likeness between these old warriors.

Presently I met another old soldier in a similar manner. He, too, did not notice me whilst I was passing.

By this time it was getting late in the afternoon, and I began to think of retracing my steps. Accordingly I turned to go back, but could see a number of tracks leading between different mounds and could not ascertain which of them I should take. In my perplexity I wanted to see someone of whom to ask the way, but could see no one. I determined to go on a few mounds further and so try to see someone – not a veteran.

I gained my object, for after going a couple of hundred yards I saw before me a single shanty such as I had seen before – with, however, the difference that this was not one for living in, but merely a roof with three walls open in front. From the evidences which the neighbourhood exhibited I took it to be a place for sorting. Within it was an old woman wrinkled and bent with age; I approached her to ask the way.

She rose as I came close and I asked her my way. She immediately commenced a conversation; and it occurred to me that here in the very centre of the Kingdom of Dust was the place to gather details of the history of Parisian rag-picking – particularly as I could do so from the lips of one who looked like the oldest inhabitant.

I began my inquiries, and the old woman gave me most interesting answers – she had been one of the tricoteuses[14] who sat daily before the guillotine and had taken an active part among the women who signalised themselves by their violence in the revolution. While we were talking she said suddenly: 'But m'sieur must be tired standing,' and dusted a rickety old stool for me to sit down. I hardly liked to do so for many reasons; but the poor old woman was so civil that I did not like to run the risk of hurting her by refusing, and

---

[14] tricoteuse: *(French) a woman who knits, this was the name given to the women who, during the French Revolution, would sit and knit while watching public executions*

moreover the conversation of one who had been at the taking of the Bastille[15] was so interesting that I sat down and so our conversation went on.

While we were talking an old man – older and more bent and wrinkled even than the woman – appeared from behind the shanty. 'Here is Pierre,' said she. 'M'sieur can hear stories now if he wishes, for Pierre was in everything, from the Bastille to Waterloo[16].' The old man took another stool at my request and we plunged into a sea of revolutionary reminiscences. This old man, albeit clothed like a scarecrow, was like any one of the six veterans.

I was now sitting in the centre of the low hut with the woman on my left hand and the man on my right, each of them being somewhat in front of me. The place was full of all sorts of curious objects of lumber, and of many things that I wished far away. In one corner was a heap of rags which seemed to move from the number of vermin it contained, and in the other a heap of bones whose odour was something shocking. Every now and then, glancing at the heaps, I could see the gleaming eyes of some of the rats which infested the place. These loathsome objects were bad enough, but what looked even more dreadful was an old butcher's axe with an iron handle stained with clots of blood leaning up against the wall on the right hand side. Still these things did not give me much concern. The talk of the two old people was so fascinating that I stayed on and on, till the evening came and the dust heaps threw dark shadows over the vales between them.

After a time I began to grow uneasy, I could not tell how or why, but somehow I did not feel satisfied. Uneasiness is an instinct and means warning. The psychic faculties are often the sentries of the intellect; and when they sound alarm the reason begins to act, although perhaps not consciously.

This was so with me. I began to bethink me[17] where I was and by what surrounded, and to wonder how I should fare

---

[15] Bastille: *Parisian fortress and prison whose storming on July 14, 1789, in a popular revolt against royal authority, marked the start of the French Revolution*

[16] Waterloo: *town in central Belgium and site of a famous battle (1815) in which British and Prussian forces defeated the French led by Napoleon*

[17] to bethink me: *(archaic) to remind myself*

in case I should be attacked; and then the thought suddenly burst upon me, although without any overt cause, that I was in danger. Prudence whispered: 'Be still and make no sign,' and so I was still and made no sign, for I knew that four cunning eyes were on me. 'Four eyes – if not more.' My God, what a horrible thought! The whole shanty might be surrounded on three sides with villains! I might be in the midst of a band of such desperadoes as only half a century of periodic revolution can produce.

With a sense of danger my intellect and observation quickened, and I grew more watchful than was my wont. I noticed that the old woman's eyes were constantly wandering towards my hands. I looked at them too, and saw the cause – my rings. On my left little finger I had a large signet and on the right a good diamond.

I thought that if there was any danger my first care was to avert suspicion. Accordingly I began to work the conversation round to rag-picking – to the drains – of the things found there; and so by easy stages to jewels. Then, seizing a favourable opportunity, I asked the old woman if she knew anything of such things. She answered that she did, a little. I held out my right hand, and, showing her the diamond, asked her what she thought of that. She answered that her eyes were bad, and stooped over my hand. I said as nonchalantly as I could: 'Pardon me! You will see better thus!' and taking it off handed it to her. An unholy light came into her withered old face, as she touched it. She stole one glance at me swift and keen as a flash of lightning.

She bent over the ring for a moment, her face quite concealed as though examining it. The old man looked straight out of the front of the shanty before him, at the same time fumbling in his pockets and producing a screw of tobacco in a paper and a pipe, which he proceeded to fill. I took advantage of the pause and the momentary rest from the searching eyes on my face to look carefully round the place, now dim and shadowy in the gloaming. There still lay all the heaps of varied reeking foulness; there the terrible blood-stained axe leaning against the wall in the right-hand corner, and everywhere, despite the gloom, the baleful glitter of the eyes of the rats. I could see them even through some of the chinks of the boards at the back low down close to the ground. But stay! these latter eyes seemed more than usually large and bright and baleful!

For an instant my heart stood still, and I felt in that whirling condition of mind in which one feels a sort of spiritual drunkenness, and as though the body is only maintained erect in that there is no time for it to fall before recovery. Then, in another second, I was calm – coldly calm, with all my energies in full vigour, with a self-control which I felt to be perfect and with all my feeling and instincts alert.

Now I knew the full extent of my danger: I was watched and surrounded by desperate people! I could not even guess at how many of them were lying there on the ground behind the shanty, waiting for the moment to strike. I knew that I was big and strong, and they knew it, too. They knew also, as I did, that I was an Englishman and would make a fight for it; and so we waited. I had, I felt, gained an advantage in the last few seconds, for I knew my danger and understood the situation. Now, I thought, is the test of my courage – the enduring test: the fighting test may come later!

The old woman raised her head and said to me in a satisfied kind of way:

'A very fine ring, indeed – a beautiful ring! Oh, me! I once had such rings, plenty of them, and bracelets and earrings! Oh! for in those fine days I led the town a dance! But they've forgotten me now! They've forgotten me! They? Why they never heard of me! Perhaps their grandfathers remember me, some of them!' and she laughed a harsh, croaking laugh. And then I am bound to say that she astonished me, for she handed me back the ring with a certain suggestion of old-fashioned grace which was not without its pathos.

The old man eyed her with a sort of sudden ferocity, half rising from his stool, and said to me suddenly and hoarsely:

'Let me see!'

I was about to hand the ring when the old woman said:

'No! no, do not give it to Pierre! Pierre is eccentric. He loses things; and such a pretty ring!'

'Cat!' said the old man, savagely. Suddenly the old woman said, rather more loudly than was necessary:

'Wait! I shall tell you something about a ring.' There was

something in the sound of her voice that jarred upon me. Perhaps it was my hyper-sensitiveness, wrought up as I was to such a pitch of nervous excitement, but I seemed to think that she was not addressing me. As I stole a glance round the place I saw the eyes of the rats in the bone heaps, but missed the eyes along the back. But even as I looked I saw them again appear. The old woman's 'Wait!' had given me a respite from attack, and the men had sunk back to their reclining posture.

'I once lost a ring – a beautiful diamond hoop that had belonged to a queen, and which was given to me by a farmer of the taxes, who afterwards cut his throat because I sent him away. I thought it must have been stolen, and taxed my people; but I could get no trace. The police came and suggested that it had found its way to the drain. We descended – I in my fine clothes, for I would not trust them with my beautiful ring! I know more of the drains since then, and of rats, too! but I shall never forget the horror of that place – alive with blazing eyes, a wall of them just outside the light of our torches. Well, we got beneath my house. We searched the outlet of the drain, and there in the filth found my ring, and we came out.

'But we found something else also before we came! As we were coming towards the opening a lot of sewer rats – human ones this time – came towards us. They told the police that one of their number had gone into the drain, but had not returned. He had gone in only shortly before we had, and, if lost, could hardly be far off. They asked help to seek him, so we turned back. They tried to prevent me going, but I insisted. It was a new excitement, and had I not recovered my ring? Not far did we go till we came on something. There was but little water, and the bottom of the drain was raised with brick, rubbish, and much matter of the kind. He had made a fight for it, even when his torch had gone out. But they were too many for him! They had not been long about it! The bones were still warm; but they were picked clean. They had even eaten their own dead ones and there were bones of rats as well as of the man. They took it cool enough those other – the human ones – and joked of their comrade when they found him dead, though they would have helped him living. Bah! what matters it – life or death?'

'And had you no fear?' I asked her.

'Fear!' she said with a laugh. 'Me have fear? Ask Pierre! But I was younger then, and, as I came through that horrible drain with its wall of greedy eyes, always moving with the circle of the light from the torches, I did not feel easy. I kept on before the men, though! It is a way I have! I never let the men get it before me. All I want is a chance and a means! And they ate him up – took every trace away except the bones; and no one knew it, nor no sound of him was ever heard!' Here she broke into a chuckling fit of the ghastliest merriment which it was ever my lot to hear and see. A great poetess describes her heroine singing: 'Oh! to see or hear her singing! Scarce I know which is the divinest'[18].

And I can apply the same idea to the old crone – in all save the divinity, for I scarce could tell which was the most hellish – the harsh, malicious, satisfied, cruel laugh, or the leering grin, and the horrible square opening of the mouth like a tragic mask, and the yellow gleam of the few discoloured teeth in the shapeless gums. In that laugh and with that grin and the chuckling satisfaction I knew as well as if it had been spoken to me in words of thunder that my murder was settled, and the murderers only bided the proper time for its accomplishment. I could read between the lines of her gruesome story the commands to her accomplices. 'Wait,' she seemed to say, 'bide your time. I shall strike the first blow. Find the weapon for me, and I shall make the opportunity! He shall not escape! Keep him quiet, and then no one will be wiser. There will be no outcry, and the rats will do their work!'

It was growing darker and darker; the night was coming. I stole a glance round the shanty, still all the same! The bloody axe in the corner, the heaps of filth, and the eyes on the bone heaps and in the crannies of the floor.

Pierre had been still ostensibly filling his pipe; he now struck a light and began to puff away at it. The old woman said: 'Dear heart, how dark it is! Pierre, like a good lad, light the lamp!'

Pierre got up and with the lighted match in his hand touched the wick of a lamp which hung at one side of the

---

[18] 'Oh!... divinest': *quotation from a poem by Elizabeth Barrett Browning entitled 'Lady Geraldine's Courtship' (1844)*

entrance to the shanty, and which had a reflector that threw the light all over the place. It was evidently that which was used for their sorting at night.

'Not that, stupid! Not that! The lantern!' she called out to him.

He immediately blew it out, saying: 'All right, mother, I'll find it,' and he hustled about the left corner of the room – the old woman saying through the darkness:

'The lantern! the lantern! Oh, that is the light that is most useful to us poor folks. The lantern was the friend of the revolution! It is the friend of the chiffonier! It helps us when all else fails.'

Hardly had she said the word when there was a kind of creaking of the whole place, and something was steadily dragged over the roof.

Again I seemed to read between the lines of her words. I knew the lesson of the lantern.

'One of you get on the roof with a noose and strangle him as he passes out if we fail within.'

As I looked out of the opening I saw the loop of a rope outlined black against the lurid sky. I was now, indeed, beset!

Pierre was not long in finding the lantern. I kept my eyes fixed through the darkness on the old woman. Pierre struck his light, and by its flash I saw the old woman raise from the ground beside her where it had mysteriously appeared, and then hide in the folds other gown, a long sharp knife or dagger. It seemed to be like a butcher's sharpening iron fined to a keen point.

The lantern was lit.

'Bring it here, Pierre,' she said. 'Place it in the doorway where we can see it. See how nice it is! It shuts out the darkness from us; it is just right!'

Just right for her and her purposes! It threw all its light on my face, leaving in gloom the faces of both Pierre and the woman, who sat outside of me on each side.

I felt that the time of action was approaching; but I knew now that the first signal and movement would come from the woman, and so watched her.

I was all unarmed, but I had made up my mind what to do. At the first movement I would seize the butcher's axe in the right-hand corner and fight my way out. At least, I would die hard. I stole a glance round to fix its exact locality so that I could not fail to seize it at the first effort, for then, if ever, time and accuracy would be precious.

Good God! It was gone! All the horror of the situation burst upon me; but the bitterest thought of all was that if the issue of the terrible position should be against me Alice would infallibly suffer. Either she would believe me false – and any lover, or anyone who has ever been one, can imagine the bitterness of the thought – or else she would go on loving long after I had been lost to her and to the world, so that her life would be broken and embittered, shattered with disappointment and despair. The very magnitude of the pain braced me up and nerved me to bear the dread scrutiny of the plotters.

I think I did not betray myself. The old woman was watching me as a cat does a mouse; she had her right hand hidden in the folds of her gown, clutching, I knew, that long, cruel-looking dagger. Had she seen any disappointment in my face she would, I felt, have known that the moment had come, and would have sprung on me like a tigress, certain of taking me unprepared.

I looked out into the night, and there I saw new cause for danger. Before and around the hut were at a little distance some shadowy forms; they were quite still, but I knew that they were all alert and on guard. Small chance for me now in that direction.

Again I stole a glance round the place. In moments of great excitement and of great danger, which is excitement, the mind works very quickly, and the keenness of the faculties which depend on the mind grows in proportion. I now felt this. In an instant I took in the whole situation. I saw that the axe had been taken through a small hole made in one of the rotten boards. How rotten they must be to allow of such a thing being done without a particle of noise.

The hut was a regular murder-trap, and was guarded all around. A garroter lay on the roof ready to entangle me with his noose if I should escape the dagger of the old hag. In front the way was guarded by I know not how many watchers. And at the back was a row of desperate men – I had seen their eyes still through the crack in the boards of the floor, when last I looked – as they lay prone waiting for the signal to start erect. If it was to be ever, now for it!

As nonchalantly as I could I turned slightly on my stool so as to get my right leg well under me. Then with a sudden jump, turning my head, and guarding it with my hands, and with the fighting instinct of the knights of old, I breathed my lady's name, and hurled myself against the back wall of the hut.

Watchful as they were, the suddenness of my movement surprised both Pierre and the old woman. As I crashed through the rotten timbers I saw the old woman rise with a leap like a tiger and heard her low gasp of baffled rage. My feet lit on something that moved, and as I jumped away I knew that I had stepped on the back of one of the row of men lying on their faces outside the hut. I was torn with nails and splinters, but otherwise unhurt. Breathless I rushed up the mound in front of me, hearing as I went the dull crash of the shanty as it collapsed into a mass.

It was a nightmare climb. The mound, though but low, was awfully steep, and with each step I took the mass of dust and cinders tore down with me and gave way under my feet. The dust rose and choked me; it was sickening, foetid, awful; but my climb was, I felt, for life or death, and I struggled on. The seconds seemed hours; but the few moments I had in starting, combined with my youth and strength, gave me a great advantage, and, though several forms struggled after me in deadly silence which was more dreadful than any sound, I easily reached the top. Since then I have climbed the cone of Vesuvius, and as I struggled up that dreary steep amid the sulphurous fumes the memory of that awful night at Montrouge came back to me so vividly that I almost grew faint.

The mound was one of the tallest in the region of dust, and as I struggled to the top, panting for breath and with my heart beating like a sledgehammer, I saw away to my left the dull red gleam of the sky, and nearer still the flashing of lights. Thank God! I knew where I was now and where lay the road to Paris!

For two or three seconds I paused and looked back. My pursuers were still well behind me, but struggling up resolutely, and in deadly silence. Beyond, the shanty was a wreck – a mass of timber and moving forms. I could see it well, for flames were already bursting out; the rags and straw had evidently caught fire from the lantern. Still silence there! Not a sound! These old wretches could die game, anyhow.

I had no time for more than a passing glance, for as I cast an eye round the mound preparatory to making my descent I saw several dark forms rushing round on either side to cut me off on my way. It was now a race for life. They were trying to head me on my way to Paris, and with the instinct of the moment I dashed down to the right-hand side. I was just in time, for, though I came as it seemed to me down the steep in a few steps, the wary old men who were watching me turned back, and one, as I rushed by into the opening between the two mounds in front, almost struck me a blow with that terrible butcher's axe. There could surely not be two such weapons about!

Then began a really horrible chase. I easily ran ahead of the old men, and even when some younger ones and a few women joined in the hunt I easily distanced them. But I did not know the way, and I could not even guide myself by the light in the sky, for I was running away from it. I had heard that, unless of conscious purpose, hunted men turn always to the left, and so I found it now; and so, I suppose, knew also my pursuers, who were more animals than men, and with cunning or instinct had found out such secrets for themselves: for on finishing a quick spurt, after which I intended to take a moment's breathing space, I suddenly saw ahead of me two or three forms swiftly passing behind a mound to the right.

I was in the spider's web now indeed! But with the thought of this new danger came the resource of the hunted, and so I darted down the next turning to the right. I continued in this direction for some hundred yards, and then, making a turn to the left again, felt certain that I had, at any rate, avoided the danger of being surrounded.

But not of pursuit, for on came the rabble after me, steady, dogged, relentless, and still in grim silence.

In the greater darkness the mounds seemed now to be somewhat smaller than before, although – for the night was closing – they looked bigger in proportion. I was now well ahead of my pursuers, so I made a dart up the mound in front.

Oh joy of joys! I was close to the edge of this inferno of dustheaps. Away behind me the red light of Paris in the sky, and towering up behind rose the heights of Montmartre – a dim light, with here and there brilliant points like stars.

Restored to vigour in a moment, I ran over the few remaining mounds of decreasing size, and found myself on the level land beyond. Even then, however, the prospect was not inviting. All before me was dark and dismal, and I had evidently come on one of those dank, low-lying waste places which are found here and there in the neighbourhood of great cities. Places of waste and desolation, where the space is required for the ultimate agglomeration of all that is noxious, and the ground is so poor as to create no desire of occupancy even in the lowest squatter. With eyes accustomed to the gloom of the evening, and away now from the shadows of those dreadful dustheaps, I could see much more easily than I could a little while ago. It might have been, of course, that the glare in the sky of the lights of Paris, though the city was some miles away, was reflected here. Howsoever it was, I saw well enough to take bearings for certainly some little distance around me.

In front was a bleak, flat waste that seemed almost dead level, with here and there the dark shimmering of stagnant pools. Seemingly far off on the right, amid a small cluster of scattered lights, rose a dark mass of Fort Montrouge, and away to the left in the dim distance, pointed with stray gleams from cottage windows, the lights in the sky showed the locality of Bicêtre. A moment's thought decided me to take to the right and try to reach Montrouge. There at least would be some sort of safety, and I might possibly long before come on some of the crossroads which I knew. Somewhere, not far off, must lie the strategic road made to connect the outlying chain of forts circling the city.

Then I looked back. Coming over the mounds, and outlined black against the glare of the Parisian horizon, I saw several moving figures, and still a way to the right several more deploying out between me and my destination. They evidently meant to cut me off in this direction, and so my choice became constricted; it lay now between going straight ahead or turning to the left. Stooping to the ground, so as to get the advantage of the horizon as a line of sight, I looked carefully in this direction, but could detect no sign of my enemies. I argued that as they had not guarded or were not trying to guard that point, there was evidently danger to me there already. So I made up my mind to go straight on before me.

It was not an inviting prospect, and as I went on the reality grew worse. The ground became soft and oozy, and now and again gave way beneath me in a sickening kind of way. I seemed somehow to be going down, for I saw round me places seemingly more elevated than where I was, and this in a place which from a little way back seemed dead level. I looked around, but could see none of my pursuers. This was strange, for all along these birds of the night had followed me through the darkness as well as though it was broad daylight. How I blamed myself for coming out in my light-coloured tourist suit of tweed. The silence, and my not being able to see my enemies, whilst I felt that they were watching me, grew appalling, and in the hope of someone not of this ghastly crew hearing me I raised my voice and shouted several times. There was not the slightest response; not even an echo rewarded my efforts. For a while I stood stock still and kept my eyes in one direction. On one of the rising places around me I saw something dark move along, then another, and another. This was to my left, and seemingly moving to head me off.

I thought that again I might with my skill as a runner elude my enemies at this game, and so with all my speed darted forwards.

Splash!

My feet had given way in a mass of slimy rubbish, and I had fallen headlong into a reeking, stagnant pool. The water and the mud in which my arms sank up to the elbows was filthy and nauseous beyond description, and in the suddenness of my fall I had actually swallowed some of the filthy stuff, which nearly choked me, and made me gasp for breath. Never shall I forget the moments during which I stood trying to recover myself, almost fainting from the foetid odour of the filthy pool, whose white mist rose ghostlike around. Worst of all, with the acute despair of the hunted animal when he sees the pursuing pack closing on him, I saw before my eyes whilst I stood helpless the dark forms of my pursuers moving swiftly to surround me.

It is curious how our minds work on odd matters even when the energies of thought are seemingly concentrated on some terrible and pressing need. I was in momentary peril of my life: my safety depended on my action, and my choice of alternatives coming now with almost every step I took, and yet I could not but think of the strange dogged persistency of these old men. Their silent resolution, their steadfast, grim, persistency even in such a cause commanded, as well as fear, even a measure of respect. What must they have been in the vigour of their youth. I could understand now that whirlwind rush on the bridge of Arcola[19], that scornful exclamation of the Old Guard at Waterloo[20]! Unconscious cerebration has its own pleasures, even at such moments; but fortunately it does not in any way clash with the thought from which action springs.

I realised at a glance that so far I was defeated in my object, my enemies as yet had won. They had succeeded in surrounding me on three sides, and were bent on driving me off to the left-hand, where there was already some danger for me, for they had left no guard. I accepted the alternative – it was a case of Hobson's choice[21] and run. I had to keep the lower ground, for my pursuers were on the higher places. However, though the ooze and broken ground impeded me my youth and training made me able to hold my ground, and by keeping a diagonal line I not only kept them from gaining on me but even began to distance them. This gave me new heart and strength, and by this time habitual training was beginning to tell and my second wind had come. Before me

---

[19] rush… Arcola: *reference to a crucial battle against the Austrians in which the French, led by Napoleon himself, took at bridge at Arcola, in Italy.*

[20] scornful…Waterloo!: *the Old Guard was the name given to the finest of the French army's elite division under Napoleon Bonaparte. Legend has it that the commander of the Old Guard reacted with scorn when, completely surrounded, they were asked to surrender at Waterloo.*

[21] Hobson's choice: *an English expression used to refer to a situation in which a person, being offered only one option, has the choice 'take it or leave it'. It is thought to originate from the practice of livery stable owner Thomas Hobson (1544-1631), who, to ensure that his horses were used in rotation, would offer customers either the horse nearest the door or no horse.*

the ground rose slightly. I rushed up the slope and found before me a waste of watery slime, with a low dyke or bank looking black and grim beyond. I felt that if I could but reach that dyke in safety I could there, with solid ground under my feet and some kind of path to guide me, find with comparative ease a way out of my troubles. After a glance right and left and seeing no one near, I kept my eyes for a few minutes to their rightful work of aiding my feet whilst I crossed the swamp. It was rough, hard work, but there was little danger, merely toil; and a short time took me to the dyke. I rushed up the slope exulting; but here again I met a new shock. On either side of me rose a number of crouching figures. From right and left they rushed at me. Each body held a rope.

The cordon was nearly complete. I could pass on neither side, and the end was near.

There was only one chance, and I took it. I hurled myself across the dyke, and escaping out of the very clutches of my foes threw myself into the stream.

At any other time I should have thought that water foul and filthy, but now it was as welcome as the most crystal stream to the parched traveller. It was a highway of safety!

My pursuers rushed after me. Had only one of them held the rope it would have been all up with me, for he could have entangled me before I had time to swim a stroke; but the many hands holding it embarrassed and delayed them, and when the rope struck the water I heard the splash well behind me. A few minutes' hard swimming took me across the stream. Refreshed with the immersion and encouraged by the escape, I climbed the dyke in comparative gaiety of spirits.

From the top I looked back. Through the darkness I saw my assailants scattering up and down along the dyke. The pursuit was evidently not ended, and again I had to choose my course. Beyond the dyke where I stood was a wild, swampy space very similar to that which I had crossed. I determined to shun such a place, and thought for a moment whether I would take up or down the dyke. I thought I heard a sound – the muffled sound of oars, so I listened, and then shouted.

No response; but the sound ceased. My enemies had evidently got a boat of some kind. As they were on the up side of me I took the down path and began to run. As I passed to the left of where I had entered the water I heard several splashes, soft and stealthy, like the sound a rat makes as he plunges into the stream, but vastly greater; and as I looked I saw the dark sheen of the water broken by the ripples of several advancing heads. Some of my enemies were swimming the stream also.

And now behind me, up the stream, the silence was broken by the quick rattle and creak of oars; my enemies were in hot pursuit. I put my best leg foremost and ran on. After a break of a couple of minutes I looked back, and by a gleam of light through the ragged clouds I saw several dark forms climbing the bank behind me. The wind had now begun to rise, and the water beside me was ruffled and beginning to break in tiny waves on the bank. I had to keep my eyes pretty well on the ground before me, lest I should stumble, for I knew that to stumble was death. After a few minutes I looked back behind me. On the dyke were only a few dark figures, but crossing the waste, swampy ground were many more. What new danger this portended I did not know – could only guess. Then as I ran it seemed to me that my track kept ever sloping away to the right. I looked up ahead and saw that the river was much wider than before, and that the dyke on which I stood fell quite away, and beyond it was another stream on whose near bank I saw some of the dark forms now across the marsh. I was on an island of some kind.

My situation was now indeed terrible, for my enemies had hemmed me in on every side. Behind came the quickening roll of the oars, as though my pursuers knew that the end was close. Around me on every side was desolation; there was not a roof or light, as far as I could see. Far off to the right rose some dark mass, but what it was I knew not. For a moment I paused to think what I should do, not for more, for my pursuers were drawing closer. Then my mind was made up. I slipped down the bank and took to the water. I struck out straight ahead, so as to gain the current by clearing the backwater of the island for such I presume it was, when I had passed into the stream. I waited till a cloud came driving across the moon and leaving all in darkness. Then I took off my hat and laid it softly on the water floating with the stream, and a second after dived to the right and struck out under water with all my might. I was, I suppose, half a minute under water, and when I rose came up as softly as I could, and turning, looked back. There went my light brown hat floating merrily away. Close behind it came a rickety old boat, driven furiously by a pair of oars. The moon was still partly obscured by the drifting clouds, but in the partial light I could see a man in the bows holding aloft ready to strike what appeared to me to be that same dreadful poleaxe which I had before escaped. As I looked the boat drew closer, closer, and the man struck savagely. The hat disappeared. The man fell forwards, almost out of the boat. His comrades dragged him in but without the axe, and then as I turned with all my energies bent on reaching the further bank, I heard the fierce whirr of the muttered 'Sacré!' which marked the anger of my baffled pursuers.

That was the first sound I had heard from human lips during all this dreadful chase, and full as it was of menace and danger to me it was a welcome sound for it broke that awful silence which shrouded and appalled me. It was as though an overt sign that my opponents were men and not ghosts, and that with them I had, at least, the chance of a man, though but one against many.

But now that the spell of silence was broken the sounds came thick and fast. From boat to shore and back from shore to boat came quick question and answer, all in the fiercest whispers. I looked back – a fatal thing to do – for in the instant someone caught sight of my face, which showed white on the dark water, and shouted. Hands pointed to me, and in a moment or two the boat was under weigh[22], and following hard after me. I had but a little way to go, but quicker and quicker came the boat after me. A few more strokes and I would be on the shore, but I felt the oncoming of the boat, and expected each second to feel the crash of an oar or other weapon on my head. Had I not seen that dreadful axe disappear in the water I do not think that I could have won the shore. I heard the muttered curses of those not rowing and the laboured breath of the rowers.

---

[22] under weigh: *under way i.e. in progress (this spelling mistake may be due to confusion with the nautical term "to weigh anchor")*

With one supreme effort for life or liberty I touched the bank and sprang up it. There was not a single second to spare, for hard behind me the boat grounded and several dark forms sprang after me. I gained the top of the dyke, and keeping to the left ran on again. The boat put off and followed down the stream. Seeing this I feared danger in this direction, and quickly turning, ran down the dyke on the other side, and after passing a short stretch of marshy ground gained a wild, open flat country and sped on.

Still behind me came on my relentless pursuers. Far away, below me, I saw the same dark mass as before, but now grown closer and greater. My heart gave a great thrill of delight, for I knew that it must be the fortress of Bicêtre, and with new courage I ran on. I had heard that between each and all of the protecting forts of Paris there are strategic ways, deep sunk roads, where soldiers marching should be sheltered from an enemy. I knew that if I could gain this road I would be safe, but in the darkness I could not see any sign of it, so, in blind hope of striking it, I ran on.

Presently I came to the edge of a deep cut, and found that down below me ran a road guarded on each side by a ditch of water fenced on either side by a straight, high wall.

Getting fainter and dizzier, I ran on; the ground got more broken – more and more still, till I staggered and fell, and rose again, and ran on in the blind anguish of the hunted. Again the thought of Alice nerved me. I would not be lost and wreck her life: I would fight and struggle for life to the bitter end. With a great effort I caught the top of the wall. As, scrambling like a catamount, I drew myself up, I actually felt a hand touch the sole of my foot. I was now on a sort of causeway, and before me I saw a dim light. Blind and dizzy, I ran on, staggered, and fell, rising, covered with dust and blood.

'Halt là!'

The words sounded like a voice from heaven. A blaze of light seemed to enwrap me, and I shouted with joy.

'Qui va là?[23]'

The rattle of musketry, the flash of steel before my eyes.

---

[23] Qui va là?: *(French) Who goes there?*

Instinctively I stopped, though close behind me came a rush of my pursuers.

Another word or two, and out from a gateway poured, as it seemed to me, a tide of red and blue, as the guard turned out. All around seemed blazing with light, and the flash of steel, the clink and rattle of arms, and the loud, harsh voices of command. As I fell forwards, utterly exhausted, a soldier caught me. I looked back in dreadful expectation, and saw the mass of dark forms disappearing into the night. Then I must have fainted. When I recovered my senses I was in the guard room. They gave me brandy, and after a while I was able to tell them something of what had passed. Then a commissary of police appeared, apparently out of the empty air, as is the way of the Parisian police officer. He listened attentively, and then had a moment's consultation with the officer in command. Apparently they were agreed, for they asked me if I were ready now to come with them.

'Where to?' I asked, rising to go.

'Back to the dustheaps. We shall, perhaps, catch them yet!'

'I shall try!' said I.

He eyed me for a moment keenly, and said suddenly:

'Would you like to wait a while or till tomorrow, young Englishman?' This touched me to the quick, as, perhaps, he intended, and I jumped to my feet.

'Come now!' I said; 'now! now! An Englishman is always ready for his duty!'

The commissary was a good fellow, as well as a shrewd one; he slapped my shoulder kindly. 'Brave garçon!' he said. 'Forgive me, but I knew what would do you most good. The guard is ready. Come!'

And so, passing right through the guardroom, and through a long vaulted passage, we were out into the night. A few of the men in front had powerful lanterns. Through courtyards and down a sloping way we passed out through a low archway to a sunken road, the same that I had seen in my flight. The order was given to get at the double, and with a quick, springing stride, half run, half walk, the soldiers went swiftly along. I felt my strength renewed again – such is the difference between hunter and hunted. A very short distance took us to a low-lying pontoon bridge across the stream, and evidently very little higher up than I had struck it. Some effort had evidently been made to damage it, for the ropes had all been cut, and one of the chains had been broken. I heard the officer say to the commissary:

'We are just in time! A few more minutes, and they would have destroyed the bridge. Forwards, quicker still!' and on we went. Again we reached a pontoon on the winding stream; as we came up we heard the hollow boom of the metal drums as the efforts to destroy the bridge were again renewed. A word of command was given, and several men raised their rifles.

'Fire!' A volley rang out. There was a muffled cry, and the dark forms dispersed. But the evil was done, and we saw the far end of the pontoon swing into the stream. This was a serious delay, and it was nearly an hour before we had renewed ropes and restored the bridge sufficiently to allow us to cross.

We renewed the chase. Quicker, quicker we went towards the dustheaps.

After a time we came to a place that I knew. There were the remains of a fire – a few smouldering wood ashes still cast a red glow, but the bulk of the ashes were cold. I knew the site of the hut and the hill behind it up which I had rushed, and in the flickering glow the eyes of the rats still shone with a sort of phosphorescence. The commissary spoke a word to the officer, and he cried: 'Halt!'

The soldiers were ordered to spread around and watch, and then we commenced to examine the ruins. The commissary himself began to lift away the charred boards and rubbish. These the soldiers took and piled together. Presently he started back, then bent down and rising beckoned me.

'See!' he said.

It was a gruesome sight. There lay a skeleton face downwards, a woman by the lines – an old woman by the coarse fibre of the bone. Between the ribs rose a long spike-like dagger made from a butcher's sharpening knife, its keen point buried in the spine.

'You will observe,' said the commissary to the officer and to me as he took out his notebook, 'that the woman must have fallen on her dagger. The rats are many here – see their eyes glistening among that heap of bones – and you will also notice' – I shuddered as he placed his hand on the skeleton– 'that but little time was lost by them, for the bones are scarcely cold!'

There was no other sign of anyone near, living or dead; and so deploying again into line the soldiers passed on. Presently we came to the hut made of the old wardrobe. We approached. In five of the six compartments was an old man sleeping – sleeping so soundly that even the glare of the lanterns did not wake them. Old and grim and grizzled they looked, with their gaunt, wrinkled, bronzed faces and their white moustaches.

The officer called out harshly and loudly a word of command, and in an instant each one of them was on his feet before us and standing at 'attention!'

'What do you here?'

'We sleep,' was the answer.

'Where are the other chiffoniers?' asked the commissary.

'Gone to work.'

'And you?'

'We are on guard!'

'Peste![24]' laughed the officer grimly, as he looked at the old men one after the other in the face and added with cool deliberate cruelty, 'Asleep on duty! Is this the manner of the Old Guard? No wonder, then, a Waterloo!'

By the gleam of the lantern I saw the grim old faces grow deadly pale, and almost shuddered at the look in the eyes of the old men as the laugh of the soldiers echoed the grim pleasantry of the officer.

I felt in that moment that I was in some measure avenged.

For a moment they looked as if they would throw themselves on the taunter, but years of their life had schooled them and they remained still.

'You are but five,' said the commissary; 'where is the sixth?' The answer came with a grim chuckle.

'He is there!' and the speaker pointed to the bottom of the wardrobe. 'He died last night. You won't find much of him. The burial of the rats is quick!'

The commissary stooped and looked in. Then he turned to the officer and said calmly:

[24] Peste!: *(French)* Here, *an exclamation: Bless my soul!*

'We may as well go back. No trace here now; nothing to prove that man was the one wounded by your soldiers' bullets! Probably they murdered him to cover up the trace. See!'

Again he stooped and placed his hands on the skeleton. 'The rats work quickly and they are many. These bones are warm!'

I shuddered, and so did many more of those around me.

'Form!' said the officer, and so in marching order, with the lanterns swinging in front and the manacled veterans in the midst, with steady tramp we took ourselves out of the dustheaps and turned backward to the fortress of Bicêtre.

* * * * *

My year of probation has long since ended, and Alice is my wife. But when I look back upon that trying twelvemonth one of the most vivid incidents that memory recalls is that associated with my visit to the City of Dust.

A DREAM OF RED HANDS

The first opinion given to me regarding Jacob Settle was a simple descriptive statement, 'He's a down-in-the-mouth[1] chap': but I found that it embodied the thoughts and ideas of all his fellow-workmen.

There was in the phrase a certain easy tolerance, an absence of positive feeling of any kind, rather than any complete opinion, which marked pretty accurately the man's place in public esteem.

Still, there was some dissimilarity between this and his appearance which unconsciously set me thinking, and by degrees, as I saw more of the place and the workmen, I came to have a special interest in him.

He was, I found, for ever doing kindnesses, not involving money expenses beyond his humble means, but in the manifold ways of forethought and forbearance and self-repression which are of the truer charities of life.

Women and children trusted him implicitly, though, strangely enough, he rather shunned them, except when anyone was sick, and then he made his appearance to help if he could, timidly and awkwardly.

He led a very solitary life, keeping house by himself in a tiny cottage, or rather hut, of one room, far on the edge of the moorland.

His existence seemed so sad and solitary that I wished to cheer it up, and for the purpose took the occasion when we had both been sitting up with a child, injured by me through accident, to offer to lend him books.

He gladly accepted, and as we parted in the grey of the dawn I felt that something of mutual confidence had been established between us.

The books were always most carefully and punctually returned, and in time Jacob Settle and I became quite friends.

Once or twice as I crossed the moorland on Sundays I looked in on him; but on such occasions he was shy and ill at ease so that I felt diffident about calling to see him. He would never under any circumstances come into my own lodgings.

One Sunday afternoon, I was coming back from a long

---

[1] down-in-the-mouth: *(colloquial) depressed, miserable*

walk beyond the moor, and as I passed Settle's cottage stopped at the door to say 'How do you do?' to him.

As the door was shut, I thought that he was out, and merely knocked for form's sake, or through habit, not expecting to get any answer.

To my surprise, I heard a feeble voice from within, though what was said I could not hear.

I entered at once, and found Jacob lying half-dressed upon his bed. He was as pale as death, and the sweat was simply rolling off his face. His hands were unconsciously gripping the bedclothes as a drowning man holds on to whatever he may grasp.

As I came in he half arose, with a wild, hunted look in his eyes, which were wide open and staring, as though something of horror had come before him; but when he recognised me he sank back on the couch with a smothered sob of relief and closed his eyes.

I stood by him for a while, quite a minute or two, while he gasped. Then he opened his eyes and looked at me, but with such a despairing, woeful expression that, as I am a living man, I would have rather seen that frozen look of horror.

I sat down beside him and asked after his health. For a while he would not answer me except to say that he was not ill; but then, after scrutinising me closely, he half arose on his elbow and said:

'I thank you kindly, sir, but I'm simply telling you the truth. I am not ill, as men call it, though God knows whether there be not worse sicknesses than doctors know of.

I'll tell you, as you are so kind, but I trust that you won't even mention such a thing to a living soul, for it might work me more and greater woe. I am suffering from a bad dream.'

'A bad dream!' I said, hoping to cheer him; 'but dreams pass away with the light – even with waking.' There I stopped, for before he spoke I saw the answer in his desolate look round the little place.

'No! no! that's all well for people that live in comfort and with those they love around them. It is a thousand times worse for those who live alone and have to do so.

What cheer is there for me, waking here in the silence of

the night, with the wide moor around me full of voices and full of faces that make my waking a worse dream than my sleep? Ah, young sir, you have no past that can send its legions to people the darkness and the empty space, and I pray the good God that you may never have!' As he spoke, there was such an almost irresistible gravity of conviction in his manner that I abandoned my remonstrance about his solitary life.

I felt that I was in the presence of some secret influence which I could not fathom. To my relief, for I knew not what to say, he went on:

'Two nights past have I dreamed it. It was hard enough the first night, but I came through it. Last night the expectation was in itself almost worse than the dream – until the dream came, and then it swept away every remembrance of lesser pain.

I stayed awake till just before the dawn, and then it came again, and ever since I have been in such an agony as I am sure the dying feel, and with it all the dread of tonight.'

Before he had got to the end of the sentence my mind was made up, and I felt that I could speak to him more cheerfully.

'Try and get to sleep early tonight – in fact, before the evening has passed away. The sleep will refresh you, and I promise you there will not be any bad dreams after tonight.'

He shook his head hopelessly, so I sat a little longer and then left him.

When I got home I made my arrangements for the night, for I had made up my mind to share Jacob Settle's lonely vigil in his cottage on the moor. I judged that if he got to sleep before sunset he would wake well before midnight, and so, just as the bells of the city were striking eleven, I stood opposite his door armed with a bag, in which were my supper, an extra large flask, a couple of candles, and a book.

The moonlight was bright, and flooded the whole moor, till it was almost as light as day; but ever and anon[2] black clouds drove across the sky, and made a darkness which by comparison seemed almost tangible.

---

[2] ever and anon: *(archaic) now and then*

I opened the door softly, and entered without waking Jacob, who lay asleep with his white face upwards. He was still, and again bathed in sweat.

I tried to imagine what visions were passing before those closed eyes which could bring with them the misery and woe which were stamped on the face, but fancy failed me, and I waited for the awakening.

It came suddenly, and in a fashion which touched me to the quick, for the hollow groan that broke from the man's white lips as he half arose and sank back was manifestly the realisation or completion of some train of thought which had gone before.

'If this be dreaming,' said I to myself, 'then it must be based on some very terrible reality. What can have been that unhappy fact that he spoke of?' While I thus spoke, he realised that I was with him.

It struck me as strange that he had no period of that doubt as to whether dream or reality surrounded him which commonly marks an expected environment of waking men.

With a positive cry of joy, he seized my hand and held it in his two wet, trembling hands, as a frightened child clings on to someone whom it loves.

I tried to soothe him: 'There, there! it is all right. I have come to stay with you tonight, and together we will try to fight this evil dream.'

He let go my hand suddenly, and sank back on his bed and covered his eyes with his hands.

'Fight it? – the evil dream! Ah! no, sir, no! No mortal power can fight that dream, for it comes from God – and is burned in here;' and he beat upon his forehead.

Then he went on: 'It is the same dream, ever the same, and yet it grows in its power to torture me every time it comes.'

'What is the dream?' I asked, thinking that the speaking of it might give him some relief, but he shrank away from me, and after a long pause said: 'No, I had better not tell it. It may not come again.'

There was manifestly something to conceal from me – something that lay behind the dream, so I answered: 'All right. I hope you have seen the last of it. But if it should come again, you will tell me, will you not? I ask, not out of curiosity, but because I think it may relieve you to speak.'

He answered with what I thought was almost an undue amount of solemnity: 'If it comes again, I shall tell you all.'

Then I tried to get his mind away from the subject to more mundane things, so I produced supper, and made him share it with me, including the contents of the flask.

After a little he braced up, and when I lit my cigar, having given him another, we smoked a full hour, and talked of many things.

Little by little the comfort of his body stole over his mind, and I could see sleep laying her gentle hands on his eyelids. He felt it, too, and told me that now he felt all right, and I might safely leave him; but I told him that, right or wrong, I was going to see in the daylight.

So I lit my other candle, and began to read as he fell asleep. By degrees I got interested in my book, so interested that presently I was startled by its dropping out of my hands.

I looked and saw that Jacob was still asleep, and I was rejoiced to see that there was on his face a look of unwonted happiness, while his lips seemed to move with unspoken words.

Then I turned to my work again, and again woke, but this time to feel chilled to my very marrow by hearing the voice from the bed beside me: 'Not with those red hands! Never! never!'

On looking at him, I found that he was still asleep.

He woke, however, in an instant, and did not seem surprised to see me; there was again that strange apathy as to his surroundings.

Then I said: 'Settle, tell me your dream. You may speak freely, for I shall hold your confidence sacred. While we both live I shall never mention what you may choose to tell me.'

He replied: 'I said I would; but I had better tell you first what goes before the dream, that you may understand.

I was a schoolmaster when I was a very young man; it was only a parish school in a little village in the West Country. No need to mention any names. Better not.

I was engaged to be married to a young girl whom I loved and almost reverenced. It was the old story. While we were waiting for the time when we could afford to set up house together, another man came along.

He was nearly as young as I was, and handsome, and a gentleman, with all a gentleman's attractive ways for a woman of our class. He would go fishing, and she would meet him while I was at my work in school.

I reasoned with her and implored her to give him up. I offered to get married at once and go away and begin the world in a strange country; but she would not listen to anything I could say, and I could see that she was infatuated with him.

Then I took it on myself to meet the man and ask him to deal well with the girl, for I thought he might mean honestly by her, so that there might be no talk or chance of talk on the part of others. I went where I should meet him with none by, and we met!'

Here Jacob Settle had to pause, for something seemed to rise in his throat, and he almost gasped for breath.

Then he went on: 'Sir, as God is above us, there was no selfish thought in my heart that day, I loved my pretty Mabel too well to be content with a part of her love, and I had thought of my own unhappiness too often not to have come to realise that, whatever might come to her, my hope was gone.

He was insolent to me – you, sir, who are a gentleman, cannot know, perhaps, how galling can be the insolence of one who is above you in station – but I bore with that.

I implored him to deal well with the girl, for what might be only a pastime of an idle hour with him might be the breaking of her heart. For I never had a thought of her truth, or that the worst of harm could come to her – it was only the unhappiness to her heart I feared.

But when I asked him when he intended to marry her his laughter galled me so that I lost my temper and told him that I would not stand by and see her life made unhappy.

Then he grew angry too, and in his anger said such cruel things of her that then and there I swore he should not live to do her harm.

God knows how it came about, for in such moments of passion it is hard to remember the steps from a word to a blow, but I found myself standing over his dead body, with my hands crimson with the blood that welled from his torn throat.

We were alone and he was a stranger, with none of his kin to seek for him and murder does not always out – not all at once.

His bones may be whitening still, for all I know, in the pool of the river where I left him.

No one suspected his absence, or why it was, except my poor Mabel, and she dared not speak.

But it was all in vain, for when I came back again after an absence of months – for I could not live in the place – I learned that her shame had come and that she had died in it.

Hitherto[3] I had been borne up by the thought that my ill deed had saved her future, but now, when I learned that I had been too late, and that my poor love was smirched with that man's sin, I fled away with the sense of my useless guilt upon me more heavily than I could bear.

Ah! sir, you that have not done such a sin don't know what it is to carry it with you. You may think that custom makes it easy to you, but it is not so. It grows and grows with every hour, till it becomes intolerable, and with it growing, too, the feeling that you must for ever stand outside Heaven.

You don't know what that means, and I pray God that you never may. Ordinary men, to whom all things are possible, don't often, if ever, think of Heaven. It is a name, and nothing more, and they are content to wait and let things be, but to those who are doomed to be shut out for ever you cannot think what it means, you cannot guess or measure the terrible endless longing to see the gates opened, and to be able to join the white figures within.

And this brings me to my dream.

It seemed that the portal was before me, with great gates of massive steel with bars of the thickness of a mast, rising to the very clouds, and so close that between them was just a glimpse of a crystal grotto, on whose shining walls were figured many white-clad forms with faces radiant with joy.

When I stood before the gate my heart and my soul were so full of rapture and longing that I forgot.

---

[3] hitherto: *up until this point*

And there stood at the gate two mighty angels with sweeping wings, and, oh! so stern of countenance. They held each in one hand a flaming sword, and in the other the latchet, which moved to and fro at their lightest touch.

Nearer were figures all draped in black, with heads covered so that only the eyes were seen, and they handed to each who came white garments such as the angels wear.

A low murmur came that told that all should put on their own robes, and without soil, or the angels would not pass them in, but would smite them down with the flaming swords.

I was eager to don my own garment, and hurriedly threw it over me and stepped swiftly to the gate; but it moved not, and the angels, loosing the latchet, pointed to my dress, I looked down, and was aghast, for the whole robe was smeared with blood.

My hands were red; they glittered with the blood that dripped from them as on that day by the river bank.

And then the angels raised their flaming swords to smite me down, and the horror was complete – I awoke.

Again, and again, and again, that awful dream comes to me. I never learn from the experience, I never remember, but at the beginning the hope is ever there to make the end more appalling; and I know that the dream does not come out of the common darkness where the dreams abide, but that it is sent from God as a punishment! Never, never shall I be able to pass the gate, for the soil on the angel garments must ever come from these bloody hands!'

I listened as in a spell as Jacob Settle spoke. There was something so far away in the tone of his voice – something so dreamy and mystic in the eyes that looked as if through me at some spirit beyond – something so lofty in his very diction and in such marked contrast to his workworn clothes and his poor surroundings that I wondered if the whole thing were not a dream.

We were both silent for a long time.

I kept looking at the man before me in growing wonderment. Now that his confession had been made, his soul, which had been crushed to the very earth, seemed to leap back again to uprightness with some resilient force.

I suppose I ought to have been horrified with his story,

but, strange to say, I was not. It certainly is not pleasant to be made the recipient of the confidence of a murderer, but this poor fellow seemed to have had, not only so much provocation, but so much self-denying purpose in his deed of blood that I did not feel called upon to pass judgment upon him.

My purpose was to comfort, so I spoke out with what calmness I could, for my heart was beating fast and heavily: 'You need not despair, Jacob Settle. God is very good, and His mercy is great. Live on and work on in the hope that someday you may feel that you have atoned for the past.'

Here I paused, for I could see that deep, natural sleep this time, was creeping upon him.

'Go to sleep,' I said; 'I shall watch with you here and we shall have no more evil dreams tonight.'

He made an effort to pull himself together, and answered: 'I don't know how to thank you for your goodness to me this night, but I think you had best leave me now. I'll try and sleep this out; I feel a weight off my mind since I have told you all. If there's anything of the man left in me, I must try and fight out life alone.'

'I'll go tonight, as you wish it,' I said; 'but take my advice, and do not live in such a solitary way. Go among men and women; live among them. Share their joys and sorrows, and it will help you to forget. This solitude will make you melancholy mad.'

'I will!' he answered, half unconsciously, for sleep was overmastering him.

I turned to go, and he looked after me. When I had touched the latch I dropped it, and, coming back to the bed, held out my hand. He grasped it with both his as he rose to a sitting posture, and I said my goodnight, trying to cheer him: 'Heart, man, heart! There is work in the world for you to do, Jacob Settle. You can wear those white robes yet and pass through that gate of steel!' Then I left him.

A week after I found his cottage deserted, and on asking at the works was told that he had 'gone north', no one exactly knew whither.

Two years afterwards, I was staying for a few days with my friend Dr Munro in Glasgow. He was a busy man, and could not spare much time for going about with me, so I spent my days in excursions to the Trossachs[4] and Loch Katrine and down the Clyde[5].

On the second last evening of my stay I came back somewhat later than I had arranged, but found that my host was late too. The maid told me that he had been sent for to the hospital – a case of accident at the gasworks, and the dinner was postponed an hour; so, telling her I would stroll down to find her master and walk back with him, I went out.

At the hospital I found him washing his hands preparatory to starting for home. Casually, I asked him what his case was.

'Oh, the usual thing! A rotten rope and men's lives of no account. Two men were working in a gasometer, when the rope that held their scaffolding broke. It must have occurred just before the dinner hour, for no one noticed their absence till the men had returned.

There was about seven feet of water in the gasometer, so they had a hard fight for it, poor fellows. However, one of them was alive, just alive, but we have had a hard job to pull him through.

It seems that he owes his life to his mate, for I have never heard of greater heroism. They swam together while their strength lasted, but at the end they were so done up that even the lights above, and the men slung with ropes, coming down to help them, could not keep them up.

But one of them stood on the bottom and held up his comrade over his head, and those few breaths made all the difference between life and death.

They were a shocking sight when they were taken out, for that water is like a purple dye with the gas and the tar.

The man upstairs looked as if he had been washed in blood. Ugh!'

'And the other?'

'Oh, he's worse still. But he must have been a very noble fellow. That struggle under the water must have been fearful; one can see that by the way the blood has been

---

[4] the Trossachs: *a wooded valley in central Scotland, lying between Loch (lake) Katrine and Loch Achray*
[5] the Clyde: *a river in Scotland*

drawn from the extremities. It makes the idea of the Stigmata[6] possible to look at him.

Resolution like this could, you would think, do anything in the world. Ay! it might almost unbar the gates of Heaven.

Look here, old man, it is not a very pleasant sight, especially just before dinner, but you are a writer, and this is an odd case. Here is something you would not like to miss, for in all human probability you will never see anything like it again.'

While he was speaking he had brought me into the mortuary of the hospital. On the bier lay a body covered with a white sheet, which was wrapped close round it.

'Looks like a chrysalis, doesn't it? I say, Jack, if there be anything in the old myth that a soul is typified by a butterfly, well, then the one that this chrysalis sent forth was a very noble specimen and took all the sunlight on its wings. See here!' He uncovered the face.

Horrible, indeed, it looked, as though stained with blood. But I knew him at once, Jacob Settle!

My friend pulled the winding sheet further down. The hands were crossed on the purple breast as they had been reverently placed by some tender-hearted person.

As I saw them my heart throbbed with a great exultation, for the memory of his harrowing dream rushed across my mind.

There was no stain now on those poor, brave hands, for they were blanched white as snow.

And somehow as I looked I felt that the evil dream was all over.

That noble soul had won a way through the gate at last. The white robe had now no stain from the hands that had put it on.

---

[6] the Stigmata: *marks, reminiscent of the wounds on the body of Christ crucified, which Christians believe may appear on the bodies of special individuals*

COMPREHENSION QUESTIONS

THE CASTLE OF THE KING
1. Explain the use of capitals in this story ('the Poet', 'Dear One', 'Beloved One', 'Her', 'the Questing Man' etc.). What effect do they have?
2. Describe how the Poet won the hand of the woman he loved.
3. Why isn't the Poet with his wife when she dies?
4. What does he decide to do on learning of her death?
5. Explain the comment 'The subtlety of the King of Death, who rules in the Realms of Evil, is great.' Provide evidence from the story to support this assertion.
6. Describe the terrifying creatures that follow the Poet's progress as he travels towards the Castle of the King. Why do they refrain from attacking him, eventually leaving him to continue his journey alone?
7. 'To the Quick alone is the horror of the passage to the Castle of the King'. What does this mean and why is this thought comforting to the Poet?
8. Why does the Poet welcome the 'terrible sound of the thunder peal'?
9. Why is it important to the dying Poet to face the King of Death on his feet?
10. What effect does the end of the story have on you?

DRACULA'S GUEST
1. Why is Herr Delbrück anxious for Johann to be back from the drive by nightfall?
2. Describe the various incidents that seem to increase Johann's fear during the drive.
3. What happened hundreds of years ago in the now deserted village that Johann refuses to visit?
4. How does Stoker convey the growing anxiety felt by the narrator as he proceeds through the valley alone?
5. The narrator, looking for shelter, is relieved when finally he sees 'some kind of building'. Why does his relief then turn to fear?
6. Describe what the narrator sees when he leans on the door of the tomb, causing it to open inwards.
7. On regaining consciousness after being hurled out into the storm, the author becomes aware of a 'heavy weight' on his chest. What is it?
8. Why are the soldiers, after saving the narrator, reluctant to refer to what they saw, and also to tell the story on their return?
9. Who sent the soldiers to look for the narrator and why?
10. Explain why, at the end of the story, the narrator feels that he is 'the sport of opposite forces'.

THE SECRET OF THE GROWING GOLD
1. Why are the Delandre and Brent families well known in the county?
2. In what ways are the two families similar to/different from each other?
3. Why is the relationship between Geoffrey Brent and Margaret Delandre difficult? Give reasons.

4. What happened to Margaret Delandre during the trip to the Continent? How did Geoffrey escape harm?
5. Why are the workmen asked to leave the hall unfinished?
6. Why does Margaret visit her brother late one night? How has she changed since he last saw her?
7. How does Geoffrey react when Margaret confronts him? (This part is not described in the story.)
8. Does Margaret exact revenge on Geoffrey? How?

THE COMING OF ABEL BEHENNA
1. Describe Abel Behenna and Eric Sanson. Who are they and how is their ancestry reflected in their looks?
2. 'They had now put the coping-stone on their Temple of Friendship'. Explain what is meant by this.
3. Why do the girls of Pencastle resent Sarah Trefusis?
4. What suggestion does Mrs Trefusis make when it becomes clear that Sarah cannot choose between Abel and Eric? What are her motives?
5. What agreement do Sarah, Abel and Eric finally reach at the Flagstaff Rock? Are they all satisfied with the decision?
6. How does Eric try to reverse his fortunes during the year of Abel's absence? How does Sarah react to Eric's attentions?
7. What do the sailors and fishermen of Pencastle do when a terrible storm blows up at sea?
8. What is the *Lovely Alice* and what happens to her?
9. Eric shows great bravery during the storm. What is the reason for his determination to help?
10. Why does Stoker liken Eric to Cain?
11. What news does the chief boatman bring?
12. The village children see a strange creature in the harbour mouth. How do they describe it?
13. Describe and explain Eric Sanson's state of mind on the morning of his wedding to Sarah Trefusis.
14. Explain the meaning of Eric's utterances at the end of the story 'Devil's help! Devil's faith! Devil's price!'

THE BURIAL OF THE RATS
1. Describe the 'work' of the Parisian rag-pickers.
2. The events of this story took place while the narrator, an Englishman, was "making a prolonged stay" in Paris. What was the reason for his stay?
3. Why does the narrator decide to investigate the way of life of the chiffonier, or rag-picker? What, if anything, will be his reward?
4. Describe the ménage inhabiting the immense old wardrobe; what most strikes the narrator about the old veterans?
5. Why does the narrator stop to talk with the old woman in the shanty? Why does he find her, and the old man Pierre, so fascinating?
6. Why does the young Englishman allow the old woman to look at his ring?
7. The old woman describes an incident, years before, in which a man met a terrible death in the Parisian sewers. How did this incident affect her?

8. According to the narrator, the old woman, in recounting this story, is conveying a series of messages to her accomplices. What are these messages?
9. Why does the narrator feel at a disadvantage when Pierre lights a lantern in the doorway of the shanty. By whom does he feel himself to be observed?
10. As he attempts to escape, negotiating dustheaps and desolate wasteland, the narrator is pursued relentlessly by the rabble from the shanty town. What is it about them, and their method of pursuit, that he finds so terrifying?
11. What causes the narrator to feel, grudgingly, a measure of respect for his pursuers?
12. How does the narrator use his hat to confound his enemies?
13. Why does he feel comforted when he hears one of them curse aloud?
14. Who eventually rescues the young Englishman?
15. What happened to the shanty?
16. How did the old woman meet her death?
17. How does the police officer insult the veterans?
18. *The Castle of the King* and *The Burial of the Rats* each describe a difficult journey undertaken by a man wishing to honour his loved one. Discuss the parallels and differences between the two stories.

A DREAM OF RED HANDS
1. Why does the narrator feel a 'special interest' in Jacob Settle, even though most people seem to regard him as rather unexceptional?
2. What is the reason for Jacob Settle's distress, and how does the narrator plan to help him?
3. How does Jacob react on awakening to find the narrator in his room? What is unusual about his reaction?
4. What terrible confession does Jacob make to the narrator?
5. Why does Jacob's dream cause him such pain, even though he has had it many times before?
6. Why does the narrator feel little inclination to judge Jacob for his crime? What advice does the he give Jacob before leaving him?
7. Describe the accident at the gasworks. What happened? How many men were involved? How many survived?
8. What is the significance of the doctor's comment: 'Resolution like this […] might almost unbar the gates of Heaven'?
9. Why does the doctor feel compelled to show the narrator the dead body lying in the mortuary?
10. Explain why the narrator exults when he sees the body, even though it is a horrible sight.

introduction, notes and exercises Frances Taylor
linguistic revision Catherine Wrenn
editing Sylvie Proser
cover
Johann Heinrich Füssli, 'Silence' (1801)

La Spiga languages

INDEX

The Castle of the King	7
Dracula's Guest	22
The Secret of the Growing Gold	35
The Coming of Abel Behenna	49
The Burial of the Rats	69
A Dream of Red Hands	95
Comprehension questions	107

• EASY READERS SELECTION •

Alcott	LITTLE WOMEN
Barrie	PETER PAN
Baum	THE WIZARD OF OZ
Bell	PLAY WITH ENGLISH GRAMMAR
Bell	PLAY WITH ENGLISH WORDS
Bell	PLAY WITH THE INTERNET
Bell	PLAY WITH... VOCABULARY
Brontë	WUTHERING HEIGHTS
Burnett	THE SECRET GARDEN
Carroll	ALICE IN WONDERLAND
Cooper	THE LAST OF THE MOHICANS
Coverley	THE CHUNNEL
Defoe	ROBINSON CRUSOE
Dickens	A CHRISTMAS CAROL
Dickens	OLIVER TWIST
Dolman	KING ARTHUR
Dolman	ROBIN HOOD STORIES
Dolman	STOLEN GENERATIONS
Dolman	THE LOCH NESS MONSTER
Dolman	THE SINKING OF THE TITANIC
Dolman	THE STORY OF ANNE FRANK
Grahame	THE WIND IN THE WILLOWS
Hetherington	THE BATTLE OF STALINGRAD
James	GHOST STORIES
Jerome	THREE MEN IN A BOAT
Kipling	JUNGLE BOOK STORIES
Leroux	THE PHANTOM OF THE OPERA
London	THE CALL OF THE WILD
London	WHITE FANG
Melville	MOBY DICK
Poe	BLACK TALES
Raspe	BARON MÜNCHHAUSEN
Scott	AMERICAN INDIAN TALES
Scott	FOLK TALES
Scott	IVANHOE
Shakespeare	ROMEO AND JULIET
Shakespeare	MIDSUMMER NIGHT'S DREAM
Shelley	FRANKENSTEIN
Spencer	THE GIRL FROM BEVERLY HILLS
Stevenson	DR JEKILL AND MR HYDE
Stevenson	TREASURE ISLAND
Stoker	DRACULA
Stowe	UNCLE TOM'S CABIN
Swift	GULLIVER'S TRAVELS
Twain	TOM SAWYER
Twain	HUCKLEBERRY FINN
Twain	THE PRINCE AND THE PAUPER
Wallace	KING KONG
Whelan	A STATUE OF LIBERTY
Whelan	DRACULA'S WIFE
Wrenn	PEARL HARBOR
Wright	DRACULA'S TEETH
Wright	ESCAPE FROM SING-SING
Wright	THE ALIEN
Wright	THE BERMUDA TRIANGLE
Wright	THE MUMMY
Wright	THE MURDERER
Wright	THE NINJA WARRIORS
Wright	THE WOLF
Wright	YETI THE ABOMINABLE SNOWMAN

• EASY READERS AUDIO ☊ •

Brontë	WUTHERING HEIGHTS
Conrad	HEART OF DARKNESS
Coverley	CALAMITY JANE • BUFFALO BILL
Demeter	HOUSE • NIGHTMARE
Dolman • Demeter	AN EXODUS • APOCALYPSE
Hapnen	STONEHENGE ENIGMA
Hartley	THE BATTLE OF BRITAIN
Hartley	WANTED DEAD OR ALIVE
Lovell	AL CAPONE • MAFIA
Marryat • Nesbit	FOREST • RAILWAY
Melville	TYPEE
Melville • London	MOBY DICK • WILD
Peet • Dolman	ORIENT • ANDES
Peet • Wright	LAWRENCE • PSYCHO
Rollasson	TROUBLE AT SCOTLAND YARD
Shakespeare	HAMLET
Shakespeare	ROMEO AND JULIET
Shelley • Wallace	FRANKENSTEIN • KING KONG
Schonbeck	EL PILAR: HEMINGWAY'S BOAT
Stoker • Poe	DRACULA • BLACK TALES
Wilde	THE PICTURE OF DORIAN GRAY
Wilde • Collins	EARNEST • MOONSTONE
Wise • Peet	LANDRU • TRAGEDY AT NIAGARA
Wright	HUNTER • CRIMINAL
Wright	JACK THE RIPPER • THE VAMPIRE

• INTERMEDIATE READERS ☊ •

Austen	MANSFIELD PARK
Austen	PRIDE AND PREJUDICE
Bell (NO CD)	PLAY with English GRAMMAR
Bell (NO CD)	PLAY with English WORDS
Bell (NO CD)	PLAY with...VOCABULARY
	BEOWULF
Brontë	JANE EYRE
Bunyan	THE PILGRIM'S PROGRESS
Chaucer	THE CANTERBURY TALES
Collins	THE WOMAN IN WHITE
Conrad	NOSTROMO
Cooper	THE LAST OF THE MOHICANS
Coverley	MY GRANDDAD JACK THE RIPPER
Defoe	MOLL FLANDERS
Eliot	THE MILL ON THE FLOSS
Fielding	JOSEPH ANDREWS
Fielding	TOM JONES
Hardy	FAR FROM THE MADDING CROWD
Hawthorne	THE SCARLET LETTER
James	THE PORTRAIT OF A LADY
James	WASHINGTON SQUARE
Jonson	THE ALCHEMIST
Lawrence	LADY CHATTERLEY'S LOVER
Lawrence	WOMEN IN LOVE
Leroux	THE PHANTOM OF THE OPERA
Richardson	PAMELA
Roberts	JOURNEY TO SAMARKAND
Roberts (NO CD)	THE HISTORY OF ENGLAND
Roberts (NO CD)	THE HISTORY OF THE USA
Thackeray	VANITY FAIR
Schreiner	STORY OF AN AFRICAN FARM
Shakespeare	ANTONY AND CLEOPATRA
Shakespeare	AS YOU LIKE IT
Shakespeare	HAMLET
Shakespeare	HENRY V
Shakespeare	KING LEAR
Shakespeare	MACBETH
Shakespeare	MUCH ADO ABOUT NOTHING
Shakespeare	OTHELLO
Shakespeare	ROMEO AND JULIET
Shakespeare	THE COMEDY OF ERRORS
Shelley	FRANKENSTEIN
Stevenson	KIDNAPPED
Stoker	DRACULA
Twain	LIFE ON THE MISSISSIPPI
Wallace	THE ANGEL OF TERROR
Wallace	THE FOUR JUST MEN
Wright	AMISTAD
Wright	BEN HUR
Wright	HALLOWEEN
Wright	RAPA NUI
Wright	THE BERMUDA TRIANGLE
Wright	THE MONSTER OF LONDON
Wright	WITNESS

• IMPROVE YOUR ENGLISH SELECTION •

Coleridge	ANCIENT MARINER
Conrad	THE INN OF THE TWO WITCHES
Dickens	☊ THE BARON OF GROGZWIG
Doyle	☊ A STUDY IN SCARLET
Doyle	TWO SHERLOCK HOLMES STORIES
Forster	A PASSAGE TO INDIA (PART II • CAVES)
James	DAISY MILLER
Kipling	JUST SO STORIES
Lamb	☊ TALES FROM SHAKESPEARE
London	THE LAW OF LIFE
Marlowe	DOCTOR FAUSTUS
Mansfield	☊ THE GARDEN PARTY
Masters	SPOON RIVER ANTHOLOGY
Maugham	THE LETTER
Orwell	THE LION AND THE UNICORN
Poe	☊ THE PIT AND THE PENDULUM
Shakespeare	☊ MACBETH
Shakespeare	☊ THE MERCHANT OF VENICE
Shakespeare	THE TEMPEST
Shakespeare	☊ TWELFTH NIGHT
Stevenson	DR JEKYLL AND MR HYDE
Stoker	☊ THE GUEST OF DRACULA
Swift	A MODEST PROPOSAL
Twain	THE £ 1,000,000 BANK NOTE
Walpole	THE CASTLE OF OTRANTO
Wilde	☊ THE CANTERVILLE GHOST
Wilde	☊ THE HAPPY PRINCE
Woolf	A HAUNTED HOUSE AND NINE OTHER STORIES
Woolf	TO THE LIGHTHOUSE (PART III • THE LIGHTHOUSE)

• POCKET CLASSICS SELECTION •

Bierce	FANTASTIC FABLES
Chesterton	THE SCANDAL OF FATHER BROWN
Conrad	HEART OF DARKNESS
Dickens	A CHRISTMAS CAROL
Dickinson	☊ SELECTED POEMS
Doyle	SHERLOCK HOLMES
Hardy	WESSEX TALES
James	THE TURN OF THE SCREW
Jerome	THREE MEN IN A BOAT
Lawrence	☊ ENGLAND, MY ENGLAND
Le Carré	CALL FOR THE DEAD
Le Fanu	☊ GHOST STORIES AND TALES OF MYSTERY
London	THE CALL OF THE WILD
London	WHITE FANG
Mansfield	IN A GERMAN PENSION
Maugham	RAIN
Melville	BILLY BUDD, SAILOR
Poe	THE MURDERS IN THE RUE MORGUE
Poe	THE NARRATIVE OF ARTHUR GORDON PYM OF NANTUCKET
Shakespeare	☊ ANTONY AND CLEOPATRA
Shakespeare	AS YOU LIKE IT
Shakespeare	☊ A MIDSUMMER NIGHT'S DREAM
Shakespeare	MUCH ADO ABOUT NOTHING
Shaw	PYGMALION
Shelley	☊ FRANKENSTEIN
Stevenson	DR JEKYLL AND MR HYDE
Stoker ☊	Selected stories of HORROR AND SUSPENSE
Twain	☊ HUMOROUS STORIES
V.A.	☊ THREE WOMEN SIX STORIES
V.A.	☊ WOMEN'S TALES OF MYSTERY
Wharton	ETHAN FROME
Whitman	LEAVES OF GRASS
Wilde	☊ AN IDEAL HUSBAND
Wilde	☊ THE IMPORTANCE OF BEING EARNEST
Wilde	THE PICTURE OF DORIAN GRAY

© 2011 ELI SRL - **LA SPIGA LANGUAGES** • TEL +39 02 2157240 • info@laspigaedizioni.it • info@elionline.com
PRINTED IN ITALY BY **TECNOSTAMPA**